A PASSION
FOR UNITY

Emilio Castro

A PASSION
FOR UNITY
Essays on ecumenical
hopes and challenges

WCC Publications, Geneva

Emilio Castro

A PASSION FOR UNITY

Essays on ecumenical hopes and challenges

WCC Publications, Geneva

Cover design: Rob Lucas

Cover photo: WCC/Peter Williams

ISBN 2-8254-1089-6

© 1992 WCC Publications, World Council of Churches,
150 route de Ferney, 1211 Geneva 2, Switzerland

Printed in Switzerland

Contents

Foreword

Almost half a century has passed since the time when Emilio Castro was one of a group of young Latin American theological students of different denominations who would have endless conversations and discussions about what should be done to renew the life and witness of our churches. On Sunday evenings when we returned from our work in the churches, in a small café a few blocks away from the Facultad Evangélica de Teología in Buenos Aires or after a vigorous football match, we mixed theology, politics, church experiences, jokes and pranks (mostly at the expense of our professors).

The unity of our churches was seldom the specific topic of those conversations. We took for granted that our churches belonged together. Years later, as ministers, we would begin to think about ways to make that unity visible and organic. We naturally participated in the Protestant Youth Federation in our countries. We knew about the ecumenical movement, but not until a few years after the war did we begin to relate ourselves personally to it in different ways, mostly through the World Student Christian Federation.

As I recollect — now probably in a more systematic way than we knew then — our thinking went back and forth between two foci. One dominant question was how to relate the gospel to the life of our societies. Some were fascinated with Emil Brunner's concept of *Anknüpfungspunkt*. Others began to explore William Temple's theological-philosophical-social articulations. Emilio turned to Reinhold Niebuhr's analysis of humanity and culture and its ethico-political implications. The other focus was our own location as *evangélicos* in Latin American culture and society, in which we wanted to deepen our roots, which were still too much attached to the missionary past.

Emilio's ministry took him to different contexts: he was pastor in Bolivia and in his native Uruguay. The impulse given by Valdo Galland to student work in Latin America enrolled us in various conferences and institutes. Emilio's passion for evangelization and gift for preaching were put to good use by many of our congregations. Soon he had the unexpected opportunity to visit the Mecca of our theological dreams. He spent one year studying in Basel with Karl Barth!

The "ecumenical movement" soon caught up with him. During his ministry in Montevideo he taught at the Mennonite Seminary and chaired the fellowship of Christians and Jews. After 1965 ecumenical ministry claimed him full-time (if there is only one full-time in a ministry like his). The long quest for a permanent ecumenical structure in Latin America, so much desired and so much feared, finally began to take shape under Emilio's coordination as UNELAM (a "provisional" committee Pro-unidad evangélica para América Latina), which eventually was reorganized as CLAI (Consejo Latinoamericano de Iglesias). He would also be called to initiate the road to cooperation in theological education through ASIT, the Latin American Association of Theological Schools, which was formed in 1965 and which he served as executive secretary until 1972. Meanwhile he had been "baptized" in the WCC's stream at the New Delhi Assembly (1961) and ever after had a vital living relation to it.

The "oikoumene" of his "passion" was never restricted to the church. The "Niebuhrian" streak of the late 1940s, theologically corrected but not erased by Barth and socially deepened and made more radical in the Latin American experience, was constantly present in his popular radio talks in Montevideo. It found further expression in the creation of ISAL (Church and Society in Latin America, 1960) and was tested in the critical moments in Uruguay in the 1970s, when he struggled to be an agent for peace and justice in the midst of conflict and violence.

Throughout all of this, while many of our churches were torn by internal debates, Emilio tried constantly to bring together — without confusion but also without separation — the passion for evangelization, for unity and for justice. That effort has a price, and often he had to suffer attacks from all fronts: too worldly for some and too pious for others; sometimes seen as too confrontational, other times as too compromising.

How can we characterize Emilio Castro's "passion for unity"? The reader will make her or his own judgement. As friend, colleague and collaborator in many ways throughout this career I would make three suggestions.

1. In all he thinks and does Emilio has a flair for the concrete. I have the impression that when he starts from a basic theological or ecclesiological foundation, he already has in mind the concrete point at which he aims to arrive. Purists will point to the dangers of theological distortion or instrumentalization in such a tendency. Contextualists will claim that there is no escape from this situation and that it is far better to acknowledge it. The question is, I think, whether the presupposed "point of arrival" can be changed, corrected or made more precise by the direction defined by the theological point of departure. I would say that he scores well in this respect. The papers collected here seem to me to bear out this judgement. They are elicited by particular situations — the question of *diakonia*, of refugees or of reconciliation in situations of conflict; or they are prompted by debates in the ecumenical movement — dialogue, evangelism or the JPIC emphasis. The addressee and the context are never forgotten, the concrete proposals become quite explicit. But the "context" is rendered open to the inspiration, the judgement and the insights of the universal "deposit of the faith".

Castro may at some point in the future write a theological treatise — perhaps now in his "retirement" — but I doubt it! I think he belongs to that race of thinkers who will not be put in motion unless they perceive a concrete challenge which has to be met. Perhaps such people do not create "eternal" works. They are more interested in discerning the points at which the "eternal" breaks into the concrete life of the world.

2. Since its definitive organization in 1948, the WCC has rendered many and noteworthy services. There is, however, one unfulfilled promise. As the Faith and Order and the Life and Work movements came together as one Council, we could expect that the quests for common witness in the the world and for church unity would become one. There have been some significant efforts (and it is not our task here to enumerate or analyze these), but the promise has not been fulfilled either structurally or theologically in the WCC. Old slogans like "doctrine divides and service unites" or "unity should not be sought for its own sake" have fortunately become obsolete. Possibly there would be agreement that the two quests should not be played

off against each other and even that they belong together as dimensions of the same gospel. We have tried to relate "the unity of the church and the unity of the human community" or spoken of the inextricable relation of "vertical" and "horizontal". But such consensus — if and to the extent that it may exist — has not become clearly visible in the concrete life of the Council or the churches.

Am I wrong in thinking that Emilio Castro's "passion for unity" has been and is a passion for *that unity*? I would dare to suggest that the coherence of the papers presented in this book could be seen in that perspective. It is interesting to see how the second essay interprets the significance of the pneumatological perspective of Canberra in terms of the relation between the koinonia of the Christian community — the quest for unity — and the work of the Spirit in the world — the quest for discernment. Or how the first paper sees the elaboration of models of unity and "the vision of the kingdom" as the expression of the same "communion in the trinitarian model". And perhaps even more interesting, the final essay, on JPIC, culminates in the significance of the concrete "covenants" in which the unity of the Christian community relates to specific historical concerns.

To what extent Emilio has been able in his time of service in Geneva, following in the tracks of many who had the same vision, to move the ecumenical movement forward on the way to the realization of what I have called "the unfulfilled promise", time will tell. That it has been a conscious purpose of his thinking and action I have little doubt.

3. A collection of Emilio's papers to honour him as he begins a new phase of his ministry could as well have been entitled "a passion for mission". Perhaps it would have led to a different selection. But I would argue that even the collection we have here could, without doing it violence, bear that title. For Castro — who is above all *un evangélical latinoamericano*, a "convert to the gospel", in the strong sense that the expression has in our churches — cannot understand a unity that is not centred in a gospel which has to be confessed, witnessed, enacted and proclaimed. When he tries to disengage interfaith dialogue from all "Enlightenment relativism" and to establish "conviction" as the basis for dialogue, or when he dares to speak of the relation to people of other faith in an address on "evangelism" he is, I think, standing on the foundation of his own personal Christian identity and risking the tension of the challenge of dialogue. It is also that "evangelical passion" which cannot think of any unity,

mission or service which does not rest in the work of the Holy Spirit in converting, sanctifying and leading, creating "new creatures" as well as "a new creation". It is this passion which makes it necessary at every point to continue to speak of a personal faith, of "personal transformation", to make preaching a permanent invitation.

It is not for me to say whether this is the Emilio Castro whom readers know, who emerges from the pages of this book or whom he recognizes himself to be. It tries to be the Emilio whom I have known, whom I respect and love, by whose ministry I, as many others, have been edified, stimulated and led — and expect and hope to continue to be edified, stimulated and led.

José Míguez Bonino

I

The Unity of the Church

The central calling of the ecumenical movement is the quest for the unity of the church. It is a quest which looks to the kingdom of God and participates in human conflicts in the name of the gospel of Jesus Christ. We are called to present the witness of a united church which can symbolize, anticipate and serve the reconciliation and unity of all humanity and the whole of creation.

Growing in the one tradition

This quest for unity involves a concerted effort to overcome great ecclesiological and doctrinal differences which are rooted in the history of the church. The churches have been drawn together in the forum constituted by the World Council of Churches because of two presuppositions which are at first sight contradictory. The first is that in God the church is a single reality and that all of us who confess the name of Jesus Christ have to work to make this reality visible. The second is that we meet as separate churches, confessions and communities, each of which claims that its liturgical and community life represents a fullness of the church which *a priori* it cannot recognize in the other church organizations.

On the one hand, we are convinced that we have to be together and grow together and move forward together because of the prayer of Jesus Christ in whom we are *already* one. On the other hand, we acknowledge that the unity we discern is *not yet* sufficient to enable us to partake together at the common table of the Lord or recognize each other's ministries or mutual reality as churches.

The ecumenical pilgrimage is a commitment to growth within the unity that already exists in God. The church is one, and our growth must be within this trinitarian reality, in which the Holy Spirit makes us one with the triune God. Our unity is growth in prayer, in common worship, in the solidarity of the cross in which the sorrow and joy of some is the sorrow and joy of the others.

The growth of the confessional families has led some people to propose the vision of a "communion of communions" as a model for the unity we seek. The encounter of these confessional families, each with its distinctive realities, would manifest the universality and catholicity of the church. But no matter how we assess this model, let us be careful not to use the term "communion" in a way that detracts from its basic theological sense of koinonia in God — a spiritual reality of a unique kind that cannot be divided into segments nor kept in watertight compartments.

We have to grow in the one tradition — communion — of the one church. We may differ about the claims of each of our churches to be the repository of that tradition, but we must affirm that this unity of the church in God exists as something made evident in a pilgrim people who celebrate, serve and confess one and the same faith, one and the same love, one and the same worship. This tradition is expressed and nourished through the text of the Bible, the common affirmation of central doctrinal truths, common liturgical celebrations and the recognition of the different gifts — ministries — God gives the church so that all may be done "in order" and "for edification" and for witness and service to the world.

On each of these elements we will have practical or conceptual divergences to overcome. But the reality of the communion that is nourished and manifested and served by these elements is present in all our churches as the evidence of God's sovereign freedom and faithfulness. We believe in the one church because God created it that way, and has promised to preserve it through the centuries. The Reformers called it the "church invisible". We are seeking to grasp and proclaim that reality and to make it visible! In the ecumenical pilgrimage we are surprised by the dawning of a unity which is nothing less than the presence of God's own self among God's own people.

We are growing in the trinitarian life, in the mystery of the joy of belonging each to each other. The real difficulty lies in the proclamation and articulation of this new reality and the relation of this living reality — both existential and ontological — with the visible authority of the churches. Ideas like conciliarity and primacy need to be analyzed and placed in the service of the primary and fundamental reality which is the common spiritual tradition in God. Thus it is essential for the WCC to call Christians to a new quest for possible forms of expressing the unity they already experience in common prayer and worship of the living God and to devote our energy and effort to describing the unity we seek and elaborating possible models for unity.

The wealth of diversity

But the unity of the church is not just the overcoming of confessional differences. It is increasingly apparent that the WCC is a place of encounter in which various expressions of the Christian faith, from the diversity of social, political and cultural contexts in which the church of Jesus Christ is rooted, meet in lively dialogue. Any WCC meeting is a forum not only for the classical confessional theological positions, but also and increasingly for the spiritual and theological currents which attempt to express the gospel faithfully in the most varied contexts. It is more and more difficult to suppose that there is a "centre" which might somehow "certify" the different cultural expressions of the faith as authentic. Instead, there is a recognition that we belong to each other in loyalty to a common tradition and, in some instances, acknowledgement of a primacy of unity that must be at the service of the missionary embodiment of the gospel in the various peoples and cultures of the world.

In the words of Nikos Nissiotis:

> It is through the local church that the catholic and universal church is made manifest in practice. The local church represents the vanguard of the latter in the world and its point of contact with the world. Every ecclesiological idea of the *ekklesia* as the mystical body of Christ becomes real through the local church in which the historical life, the liturgy, the missionary, charitable, catechetical and social activities take place. As part of the one catholic church, the local church possesses the fullness of the grace and of the truth of Christ, because of the presence of the qualitative idea of catholicity ("La présence dynamique et la mission de l'Eglise locale dans le monde d'aujourd'hui", Chambésy, 1981).

The novelty here is not the cultural diversity of Christianity itself, but the explosion of this diversity and our awareness of it, thanks to increased travel and communication. The New Testament already displayed this contextual richness of the gospel in the accounts of Peter's encounter with Cornelius and of the travels of Paul, the evangelist to the Gentiles. Cyril and Methodius struggled mightily to preserve the culture of the Slavic peoples while introducing them to the gospel of Jesus Christ. The peoples of Central and Eastern

Europe today are able to worship God in terms of their own heritage because of those pioneers who affirmed not just the right but the duty of every mission to forge links with national realities.

Today we see this wealth of the gospel manifested in the situation of the church in diaspora and mission throughout the world. For some this raises fears of anarchy, of diversity so great that it might obscure the central Christian substance, of the apparent disintegration of a unity that has come about through the centuries and which is central to their idea of the church. Others are concerned about the possibilities of untamed nationalism, blessed in the name of the Christian faith, creating conflict between nations. But it is precisely the ecumenical encounter on a worldwide scale that enables us to take precautions against these dangers — dangers which do not arise where minority churches oppose the powers-that-be and call for justice for the poor and marginalized, but when these same churches come to be part of the structures of power and unthinkingly retain a theological rhetoric that was appropriate to a situation of weakness but in association with power turns them into sectarians and imperialists.

The embodiment of the gospel in different cultures is not in the first instance a danger. It is above all a responsibility to leaven society as a whole with the leaven of the Christian gospel. It is a missionary responsibility to succeed in becoming all things to all people so that the gospel can speak authoritatively to the soul and the culture of every people. When we seek the unity of the church we are seeking the harmony of all these riches in a disciplined and enthusiastic ecumenical dialogue, in which all churches will inspire and be inspired, correct and be corrected.

The World Council of Churches takes on new importance as an international forum in which all paternalist pretensions are censured and we are challenged to overcome our provincial limitations in dialogue with the experience of the church of Jesus Christ in the most varied circumstances. Any model of visible unity for the church must acknowledge the wealth of this diversity and ensure that each local church has pastoral and missionary freedom.

Churches and movements

A third dimension of the unity we seek is that produced by the encounter between churches as formal, canonical institutions and movements in which Christians serve particular specialized visions of witness and Christian obedience. Movements for mission, social concern, service, education and doctrinal unity that have been incorporated into the life of the WCC continue to be fruitful realities which must be acknowledged, nourished and used in the total quest for the unity of the church.

The WCC is fundamentally a structure accountable to the organized churches. That is where the basis for its existence lies, where the permanent point of reference or centre of authority is to be found, where the people of God we want to serve meet together. But that people of God has adopted a rich variety of forms to meet challenges in many different fields — ecology, peace, justice, mission, culture, art and so on. Each of these manifestations of the church must be drawn into an ongoing dialogue in which its vitality is confronted by the traditional coherence of the Christian revelation and its challenge or protest is received as a service rendered to the fullness of the people of God. In this encounter the voluntary groups are not only recognized for the importance of the particular frontier situation in which they serve, but also compelled to look towards the future, to the permanent existence of the church of Jesus Christ and its witness through the generations.

Ecumenical movements at the base, in slum quarters and in parishes, represent a ferment, a gentle but necessary pressure pushing the church at all levels to live out the quest for Christian unity more zealously and with a greater sense of urgency. We must avoid such false contrasts as the idea that church authorities are always conservative while voluntary movements are always progressive. Those entrusted with the responsibility of authority in the church and dedicated to it are trying to interpret God's will for the total witness of the church. Organized voluntary movements within the churches fulfill an absolutely necessary function which will be doubly useful if they remain in a dynamic, dialectical relationship of criticism and cooperation with all levels of church's life. Here, too, correction and mutual inspiration is the special genius of the ecumenical movement and a vital experience in the life of the World Council of Churches.

It can be observed that the churches have gradually taken on greater responsibility for the progress of the Council and with that greater authority. This in itself is a healthy ecumenical step forward. But this greater participation and responsibility of the official church must not diminish the vitality that comes through contacts with the thousands of voluntary Christian groups who are trying to put

Christian obedience into practice in particular frontier situations. The health of the WCC and the ecumenical movement as a whole depends on using its creative imagination to find liberating and responsible ways to maintain this relationship. The WCC's emphasis on the participation of women and young people and the call for a balance of the geographical and cultural elements which make it a *World* Council of Churches are rooted in a recognition of the reality of the church which is within our church communities and which must also have the opportunity to reveal itself in the quest for unity.

Again, the emphasis on seeking access to all the gifts of the church community is not new. The preparatory committee which organized the First Assembly said the new Council must "leave the door open wide for the contributions of individual men and women who as laymen or as theologians have the special gifts of prophetic vision and discernment which are required for the building of the ecumenical fellowship and the passing on of its witness." What is new as the years have passed is the insistence that gifts of wisdom and vision exist in sectors of the church which have not usually been included in its decision-making centres. Hence the gentle but persistent pressure on the churches to include in their official delegations representatives of minorities, women, youth, laypeople, parish ministers.

This development has not been without problems, which are beginning to raise questions about the WCC's reality as a council of churches. If participation is only a kind of arithmetical game, we may achieve a sociological representation of the church without representation of those whom the churches recognize as their own leaders and spokespersons. We must use our imagination to the full to discover structures which enable us to receive the contributions of all sectors of the people of God while at the same time acknowledging the special authority which the churches, through their normal decision-making mechanisms, have granted to individuals within them.

If we are optimists, we will expect this problem to diminish as women and young people are increasingly recognized within the member churches and it becomes the norm for them to represent authoritative bodies in their churches. But since these processes occur at different tempos, more rapidly in the WCC than in the individual churches, we must think of creative alternatives which preserve the riches we have gained from full participation of women and young people in the governing bodies of the WCC and still allow us to benefit from the experience and support of the leaders appointed by the churches.

The WCC and non-member churches

The ecumenical movement is much wider than the World Council of Churches. Yet if the WCC is to serve more effectively the movement for the visible unity of the church, it must broaden the spectrum of participants, for a significant part of worldwide Christianity does not yet see itself as having a place within the WCC family.

Since 1948 we have been delighted to see all the Orthodox churches in the world become full members of the WCC, thus answering the prophetic call of the Ecumenical Patriarchate in 1920. We have seen growing participation by the churches of the Third World, not only numerically but also in theological and spiritual vitality.

But the challenge is still before us. Within the confessional families are churches which have not felt motivated to be directly involved in ecumenism beyond their own tradition. Likewise the regional ecumenical organizations add to the ecumenical circle through the participation of churches still not members of the WCC. Especially in Africa and Latin America many independent and Pentecostal churches have come into being. They are marked by special enthusiasm and by difficulties in defining doctrine, but they are a reality of the people gathered round the symbols of the Christian faith. With their vitality and fresh experience of the gospel they could contribute to the whole ecumenical dialogue while at the same time benefitting from contact with the historical tradition of the Christian churches.

One problem needs special attention. Hundreds of churches have a membership below the limits laid down in the WCC Constitution. We acknowledge the fear expressed by Orthodox friends who say that constant addition of Protestant member churches will inevitably reduce the presence in the Council of the Orthodox churches, which by definition do not create new churches. Some would even say that acceptance of many churches as members, especially those produced by divisions within other churches, is a step in the opposite direction from the basic calling to unity. But the primary concern here is a pastoral one. These small churches are a reality. Some are in isolated situations; many are growing swiftly. It would be an ecumenical service to help them to see themselves as members of a much larger family, to include them in processes of unity and so begin to correct the present splintering. A more regional emphasis in the WCC's work could free energies for a more dynamic and creative pastoral relationship with the many small churches which are on the one hand contributing to the worldwide proclamation of the gospel but can on the other hand, if left in isolation, turn into sectarian bodies which disrupt the unity we seek and for which Christ prayed.

From the start there have been a certain number of churches which reject the conciliar path as a means of expressing unity. Perhaps they have never had the chance to revise this initial decision. The WCC has indirect relations with several of these churches through the Christian World Communions and national and regional ecumenical organizations. Some theologians representing these traditions participate in Faith and Order. But we have not yet been able to open a new dialogue to overcome the initial misunderstandings. Here is another ecumenical service the WCC can render.

Since the Uppsala Assembly in 1968 the question of the membership of the Roman Catholic Church in the WCC has been open. The official response given by Pope Paul VI at that time is well known: "We do not consider that the question. . . is so mature that a positive answer could or should be given. The question still remains an hypothesis. It contains serious theological and pastoral implications. It thus requires profound study and commits us to a way that honesty recognizes could be long and difficult."

Quite apart from the issue of membership, it must be acknowledged that the collaboration of the Roman Catholic Church in the work of the WCC has followed an upward curve. To be sure, there have been peaks and troughs, but a host of services and dialogues have resulted which are a real blessing. And even if Roman Catholic membership of the WCC seems unlikely in the foreseeable future, the primates of two WCC member churches — the late Ecumenical Patriarch Dimitrios I in 1987 and Archbishop of Canterbury George Carey in 1992 — have publicly expressed the hope for such a step during visits to WCC headquarters.

The mission of the World Council of Churches is by definition worldwide; its calling is universal. When it looks beyond itself to churches which have not joined, its intention is not merely to invite them to become part of something that already exists. It is an appeal to join the search for the most useful ways to serve the ecumenical cause. And the Council itself must be open to the possibility that changes in its own structure may be necessary to facilitate this involvement in a wider forum and fuller service in the cause of the unity of the church.

Unity in the midst of history

The search for the unity of the church cannot be located outside history. It is not merely an intellectual exercise of comparing doctrines in the hope of overcoming differences, but it is an effort to discover the form of Christian obedience that is appropriate for our times.

We cannot ignore history because the divisions that reveal themselves in doctrinal and canonical divergences have historical, social, political and cultural roots. But the central reason for locating the theme of unity among human conflicts is that this is where the biblical vision locates it. The aim of history revealed in Jesus Christ, according to the letter to the Ephesians, is "to gather up all things in him" (Ephesians 1:10). The vision in Revelation 21 of a new Jerusalem, a new heaven and a new earth, speaks to us of the transformation of the whole of reality. The people of faith, the church, is called as a witness to the saving and liberating purpose of God for all creation (Ephesians 3:8-11). The unity to which the Lord calls us is a unity for the benefit of the world, so that the world may believe (John 17:21). The church is called as a priestly people to intercede for the salvation of the whole world (1 Peter 2:9). The one church is a parable and a reality anticipating the one humanity. It is an encouragement for every attempt to overcome any of the barriers which divide humanity.

In the experience of the World Council of Churches, this encounter between the quest for the unity of the church and the vision of the kingdom of God as the aim of our efforts takes place within the actual conflicts which divide humanity, ensuring a continuing tendency to disagreement and controversy in ecumenical life. Our journey takes place in the midst of the sunshine and shadow of efforts to be obedient to the heavenly vision. Thus the World Council has placed itself in the service of peace. This seems logical for those who think of themselves as following the Prince of Peace. Already at Amsterdam a central consideration was the need to ensure peace between the great power blocs of East and West. But Amsterdam also revealed the limitations of the WCC in this area. It had little to say about Palestine in the year when its partition took place and nothing about the conflict between the Netherlands, the host country for the Assembly, and Indonesia.

We acknowledge that there is ambiguity in our choice of human conflicts. Sometimes this results from our ignorance of facts or the limitation of our perspectives. More often it is a consequence of pastoral considerations. The WCC always offers a *public* platform, where criticisms are welcome as they help us to remain constantly watchful — even in situations when the criticisms are unjust and we cannot answer them, because silence is the best way to serve peace in that situation.

When we adopt positions which we think point towards the kingdom of God and show solidarity with those who are suffering, we constantly run the risk of division. We are comforted to see that at times history vindicates controversial positions taken by the World Council. But even before such vindication, the discussions within the WCC offer a unique service, as delegates speak in freedom across ideological barriers in impassioned but respectful debate and struggle to a conclusion which, though it may seem to satisfy no one fully at the time, anticipates a later resolution of the problem.

Our unity will continue to be tested as we are confronted by future areas of disagreement. Will we have the courage to affirm that all war is anti-Christian? Jacques Ellul criticized the Amsterdam Assembly for not having the courage to speak clearly about non-violence as the only possible way for humanity. The credibility of the gospel is at stake in our service for peace. The fact that our unity in the ecumenical family has been able to resist and overcome divergences on how to address the conflicting factors in different situations invites us to believe that together we dwell in the love of God in the mystery of the Trinity.

The WCC has also encouraged the proclamation of the gospel by its member churches, recognizing that the message of reconciliation has been entrusted to the churches for proclamation throughout the world (2 Corinthians 5:18-21). But the message of reconciliation in Jesus Christ's way, following the model of the cross, obliges us to take sides on behalf of the poor and the weak. No reconciliation can be brought about from a position of distance, neutrality or neglect. Work for reconciliation starts with suffering and identification. Therefore proclaiming reconciliation always requires costly solidarity.

Perhaps in the history of the WCC the most vivid example of the impact of participation in human conflicts on the quest for unity has been provided by the Special Fund to Combat Racism. There has never been controversy about the purpose of the struggle against racism, nor about solidarity with the churches and people suffering from racial oppression. But the methodology for engaging in this struggle and expressing this solidarity can be and often is controversial. Yet again and again WCC Assemblies and Central Committees have decided to risk controversy and ambiguity to make it absolutely clear that unity in Christ is unity in hope with the oppressed and the poor. Unity within and between the churches of the World Council of Churches has to be linked with the ecumenical responsibility of judging all realities from the standpoint of the coming kingdom, the saving purpose of God.

Diakonia, Christian service, has been a constant dimension in the search for the unity of the churches in the World Council of Churches. Christians cannot seek to unite or celebrate their unity without facing the world and trying to meet its needs. Without accepting naively the old slogan that "doctrine divides, service unites", we must be grateful that the possibility and reality of mutual service have become important instruments in the growth of trust, the display of mutual love and better service to the world. Common witness through our proclamation and our service reflects the unity that already exists and nourishes the unity we seek. At the same time we must be prepared to find ourselves in situations where the type of services we feel called to offer creates controversy and even division among the churches. Our unity is strong enough to generate service to humanity. It must also be strong enough to stand up to disagreements on the type of service to be given and to engender a degree of trust which will allow us to have confidence that the aims we are pursuing are the same, even when our methods may temporarily be opposed.

For example, there is the issue of service to human rights victims in situations of dictatorship. How can we best serve the victims but also ensure the ministry of the church in such countries? In Latin America we have sometimes faced, if not conflicts between the churches, then at least serious differences in the pastoral emphases appropriate in particular circumstances. Another example arises when we are confronted by forms of diakonia addressed to the situation of interdependence prevailing in the world of today, such as the condemnation of foreign debt or of the complicity of our economic systems in oppressive situations. Here we shall be setting standards of service in which we shall not always agree as to the handling of information and the methods used.

The unity of the church will be a parable of the unity God is preparing for his creation insofar as it faces reality, embraces historical conflicts and sets its course by the coming kingdom, the love kindled in the heart through its relationship with the living Christ, and the fervent hope which is the fruit of the presence of the Holy Spirit in the community of believers.

* * *

What we have learned in the quest for unity in the service of God's eschatological plan raises challenging questions about the community which the WCC constitutes and its capacity for service. Let me sum up by mentioning a number of areas on which I believe the WCC must focus in the years ahead:

● We need to recover a passion for unity, discerning in the depth of our faith its demand that we recognize that being in Christ implies being with others and for others. Every aspect of every WCC programme must be seen as serving this vision, passion and conviction.

● We need to progress in the quest for models to express the growing reality of our common belonging to the same ecclesial tradition. This means giving content to the idea of conciliar communion and placing on the agenda for discussion the relation between the perennial tradition of the church and the exercise of authority in the actual churches — not just as a theological problem about the recognition of holy orders, but as a practical recognition of the type of authority needed to acknowledge, serve and celebrate existing unity.

● In all the dimensions we have mentioned, a closer and more direct relation with and among the churches is essential. The WCC's working structure enables it to adopt a prophetic stance, serving the churches by generating ideas and challenges to them. But we must also listen more closely to what the Holy Spirit is already doing within each church community.

● We need to deepen the eschatological vision of the coming kingdom as support and inspiration for our ecumenical pilgrimage. This does not mean simply projecting things into the future or postponing the possibility of church unity till the coming of the kingdom of God. Eschatology is an anticipation, an earnest of the promise of that kingdom in the presence of the Lord of the church, in the receiving of the Holy Spirit. The eschatological vision of the reuniting of all things in Christ is the inspirational model, the object of our efforts and God's promise for the ecumenical task.

• We need to maintain watchfulness in prayer, the invocation of the Holy Spirit, because the unity of the church and service to the world are miracles of God. We began by affirming the enduring tradition of the church, the faithfulness of God, the reality of being the church in the mystery of the Trinity itself. The experiences of the WCC have confirmed again and again the faithfulness of the Holy Spirit. We have learned to live out the tension of our separation in the expectation of its being overcome through the action of the Spirit of God. We have learned to live in *epiklesis*, in the permanent invocation of a presence which alone is capable of guaranteeing the WCC's place in the perennial tradition of the church, in its fundamental reality in the triune God.

II

Come, Holy Spirit — Renew the Whole Creation

The choice of the theme "Come, Holy Spirit — Renew the Whole Creation" for the WCC's Seventh Assembly in Canberra, 1991, focussed ecumenical theological reflection and worship on the person and work of the Holy Spirit. Many were enthusiastic about the selection of this theme, believing the time had come to enlarge our trinitarian understanding and reflection after many years of concentration on the work and person of Jesus Christ. Others expressed concern about losing precisely the Christological anchorage of the WCC. But all agreed that a deeper reflection on the holy Trinity could help in the search for vitality and coherence in ecumenical theology and for understanding and relating to God's grace and work in church, creation and history.

In what follows, I will select a few points of concentration on which I believe the Seventh Assembly recognized our being together under the inspiration of the Holy Spirit. Much of this, of course, is the crowning of years of theological thought and programmatic work in the churches. But Canberra was a moment in which, because we were invited to concentrate on the person and work of the Holy Spirit, we came to an awareness that led to common affirmations and opened the way to growth in our exploration of Christian truth and obedience.

The search for the unity of the church in koinonia

The Holy Spirit draws churches into relationships of love and commitment. The Holy Spirit calls the churches to an increased commitment to the search for visible unity and more effective mission. We urge the churches to heed the call of the Spirit, to seek new and reconciled relationships between peoples, and to use the gifts of all their members.

We ourselves, the churches in council, still experience brokenness. Reconciliation between churches remains incomplete. However, in the ecumenical movement, we have been enabled to come out of isolation into a committed fellowship: we experience a growing responsibility for each other, in joy and in pain, and under the guidance of the Holy Spirit we seek ways to be more accountable to one another and to our Lord who prayed that we "may be one" (John 17:20). But we also recognize that the fullness of reconciliation is a gift of God and that we can appropriate it only insofar as the Holy Spirit transforms and sanctifies us (Assembly Message, pp. 2-3).*

Reading the reports produced by the Assembly sections and committees, one is impressed by the renewed momentum of urgency, even sense of impatience in relation to the unity of the church. Almost every report puts this as central to the attention of the churches and to the vocation of the World Council of Churches. "The Holy Spirit as promoter of koinonia (2 Corinthians 13:13) gives to those who are still divided the thirst and hunger for full communion. We remain restless until we grow together according to the wish and prayer of Christ that those who believe in him may be one" (Reference Committee, p. 174).

This urgency for the unity of the church comes from two sources. One is the growing awareness of the sacramental, symbolic and instrumental value of the unity of the church to serve the purpose of God to gather the whole of creation under the lordship of Jesus Christ. "The church is the foretaste of this communion with God and with one another," says the statement on "The Unity of the Church as Koinonia: Gift and Calling" (p. 172). A foretaste is a provocation for something more. Because we anticipate the promises of the *una sancta*, we are eager to be together at the common table of the Lord. The other source is an awareness that the credibility of the church's testimony is at stake. In a world in which the reconciling vocation of the church is more necessary than ever, we cannot offer wise or pious counsel to warring factions in humanity without showing that we can overcome our own historical divisions and provide a parable of the potential reconciliation of every human conflict.

---

* Quotations from Seventh Assembly documents are taken from the official report, *Signs of the Spirit*, ed. by Michael Kinnamon (Geneva: WCC Publications, 1991). The name of the report and the page reference are included in parentheses in the text.

Under the guidance of the Holy Spirit we have recognized that the unity we seek is fundamentally a koinonia, a communion in God with one another. Its nature is profoundly spiritual, liturgical. According to Jesus' words, it is unity "in us", meaning in God in the Trinity (John 17:20).

The cry for eucharistic sharing expresses a kind of nostalgia for the total presence of God in our life. It manifests the conviction that just as the *epiklesis*, the invocation of the Holy Spirit in the holy eucharist, is a call for the transformation of the supper in the actual reality of the living Christ, the calling for the Holy Spirit in relation to the unity of the church could also be responded to in the same mystery of communion of love. The impatience for unity is the same spiritual expectation that is present when the elements of the eucharist are raised in front of the people of God, and the priest and the people call on the Spirit to come, so that the miracle happens.

This anticipation is coming to the forefront of ecumenical consciousness. But spiritual unity does not mean invisible unity, or unity aside from the conflicts of history. "In the ecumenical movement the churches walk together in mutual understanding, theological convergences, common suffering and common prayer, shared witness and service as they draw close to one another. This has allowed them to recognize a certain degree of communion already existing between them. This is indeed the fruit of the active presence of the Holy Spirit in the midst of all who believe in Christ Jesus and who struggle for visible unity now" (Reference Committee, p. 173). The unity we seek is one that involves all levels of our life as churches of Jesus Christ. This is the vision required to respond to the WCC's first function to call the churches to the goal of *visible* unity, but this visible unity should express the depth of our spiritual communion in the mystery of the Triune God.

This recentering on the search for the visible unity of the church brings some challenges and tasks. The first is to grow steadily in the doctrinal spelling out of the communion which already exists, in the articulation of our common faith. In so doing we will keep in mind what was said by the New Delhi Assembly in 1961: "Intellectual formulations of faith are not to be identified with faith itself, and koinonia in Christ is more nearly the precondition of 'sound doctrine' than vice versa. The primary basis of this koinonia is the apostolic testimony in the holy scriptures and 'the hearing of faith'. Yet this primary biblical revelation was given to and through the apostolic church and has continued to be witnessed to by our common historic creeds, specifically the Apostles' Creed and the Nicaeo-Constantinopolitan Creed." So our search for doctrinal unity should be carried on in an atmosphere of prayer, contemplation and adoration. Faith requires understanding. In this give and take of liturgical celebration and theological reflection we grow together to be able to confess the apostolic faith today.

Many bilateral dialogues provide an excellent service in overcoming specific difficulties between different churches, thus contributing to the historical rebuilding of the *una sancta*. The specific responsibility of the World Council of Churches is to search for the expression of our common faith in a *pluralistic* engagement. In fact, there are no pure bilateral engagements. All churches are already permeated by the ecumenical movement, and there is a growth of reciprocal recognition. This means that a dialogue between Methodists and Orthodox, for example, will have consequences for dialogue between Methodists and Baptists and between Orthodox and Pentecostals. The World Council of Churches must concentrate on producing the climate of doctrinal convergence that will feed bilateral dialogues and keep them accountable to the whole household of faith.

A second concentration point for our work should be the effort to discover the *one tradition* in our different church traditions. In God's perspective, there is only one church, and the Holy Spirit has granted gifts to that church. What we see today are different expressions of that church, but these different expressions are not yet ready to recognize all the others as being full churches. But we are not trying to build a unity that will produce something that did not exist before. Rather, we are trying to discover afresh the common tradition that is the foundation stone of all our churches, to be able to recognize the quality of being church, the transcendence of our community life that imposes reciprocally the recognition of the presence and mystery of God in each particular expression of the body of Christ.

We would like to see something more — that within each of our churches the full presence of the Spirit of God, the realization of the body of Christ, is perceived as a reality so that together we could celebrate the common tradition and be open for reciprocal inspiration and correction. Practically, this means that expressing solidarity, making ecumenical visits, sharing worship, exchanging liturgical and musical resources — in short, opening ourselves to one another — are essential for our ecumenical pilgrimage. The recent step towards reciprocal recognition taken by the two Orthodox families is a good illustration of what we are trying to develop. By being able to discuss and pray together, they came to recognize in each other's family the reality of the mystery of God's presence and could affirm that their doctrinal divergences were historical misunderstandings of the deeper unity that was real in God. The next step is to develop fully the pastoral dimension of their unity. That means involving the whole people of God in the affirmation of their reciprocal recognition. This is essential in ecumenical work.

A consensus document like *Baptism, Eucharist and Ministry*, important as it is, means very little if it does not become part of the common mind of the people of God, if it is not appropriated by the members of the churches. What we call ecumenical formation is precisely the development of a reciprocal knowledge and awareness of the common tradition from which we all receive our inspiration and direction. Ecumenical formation looks forward to overcoming the ignorance and caricatures of each other which have created the heritage of mutual polemics. Involving the whole people of God is essential so that the questions which are central to their spiritual experience will challenge and encourage our theological dialogue.

Finally, we need to work on the concept and reality of koinonia to see how it helps us to describe the style and quality of the unity we seek. As the relation of love produces a freely consumed *perichoresis* (co-inherence) in the holy Trinity, so love as the source of authority in the church and among churches should eliminate all categories of power and all relations of reciprocal fear. The richness of the concept of conciliar fellowship is that it includes the dimension of love and freedom that will manifest itself in solidarity, inspiration, correction and accountability.

The Spirit at work in the world

> We pray that the Spirit of God may lead Christians to a renewed vision of God's rule, so that we may be empowered to assume the stewardship of the "mystery of the gospel" (Ephesians 6:19). We pray that we may be enabled to bear the "fruit of the Spirit" and thus witness to God's rule of love and truth, righteousness and justice and freedom, reconciliation and peace (Assembly Message, p. 3).

The theme of the Canberra Assembly was an invitation to explore the presence and action of the Holy Spirit in all creation, outside as well as inside the church. As Krister Stendahl has written, "When we call on the Holy Spirit to renew the whole creation, we become aware that God's Spirit permeates the whole cosmos and the whole oikoumene in ways which cannot be controlled or manipulated by us. The Spirit surely 'bloweth where it listeth' (John 3:8). That has always been disconcerting to orderly religious souls. . . Jesus said: Those who are not against us are for us (Mark 9:38-41). We quote the opposite saying more often. We seem to like the *or* more than the *and*.

"The Holy Spirit, the one and ever same eternal Spirit, will enable us to think 'both-and' in many situations where we excel in 'either-or'. We shall become familiar with the ways in which:

● "The Spirit as Teacher renews the faith of the church *and* the intellectual quest of humanity;

● "The Spirit as Unifier renews the love of the church *and* the solidarity of humanity;

● "The Spirit as Liberator renews the justice of the church *and* the moral energy of humanity;

● "The Spirit as Vivifier renews the hope of the church *and* the aspirations of humanity".*

This freedom of the Spirit is protected in the original wording of the creed — "We believe in the Holy Spirit, the Lord and Giver of life, who proceeds from the Father" — without the addition of the *filioque*, "from the Son". The Assembly affirmed the presence of the Spirit both in holding creation as life and in promoting renewal and change in history. The Assembly based its reflections on theological references to the church fathers, both those who taught the *logos spermatikos*, the presence of the seeds of the logos of God in all of creation, and those who spoke of the *energeia*, the uncreated energies of God at work to preserve the whole of creation.

The *energeia* of the Spirit works towards the *theosis*, the transformation, the eschatological fulfillment of creation in the kingdom to come. This basic theological understanding of the action of the Holy Spirit in creation provides an expectation for every encounter with the world outside the church. The belief that the Spirit is at work explains a certain optimism prevalent in ecumenical documents. We are going to the encounter of the living God who sustains and renews. Of course, the centrality of the cross of Jesus Christ is a reminder of

---

* *Energy for Life*, Geneva: WCC Publications, 1990, pp. 49f.

the reality of evil in the world. We cannot be naive. But the resurrection faith is stronger than our fear of sin. The action of the Spirit encourages us to look for the seven thousand faithful who have not surrendered to Baal (1 Kings 19:18).

The two speakers on the main theme in Canberra highlighted this freedom of the Holy Spirit. Patriarch Parthenios said: "All things are sanctified by the Holy Spirit, from the beginning of creation, when he hovered over the abyss, and now in nature, in heaven and on earth, in humanity, in all beings, in every living soul. . . Our witness is one of mission and dialogue. All tongues, nations, races, sexes, all kindreds, tribes and peoples *are God's*. They should be free. We must strive for their freedom. This is our ministry in the Holy Spirit, always and everywhere. Our dialogue with other religions and ideologies has the same basis. Our goal is the unity of the world. Such unity is not alien to the work of the Holy Spirit and the church. The Spirit blows where he wills, and we have no right, nor is it an act of love, for us to restrict his movement and his breathing, to bind him with fetters and barbed wire" (The Theme, pp. 31, 16).

Something similar was affirmed by Professor Chung: "The spirit of this compassionate God has been always with us from the time of creation. God gave birth to us and the whole universe with her life-giving breath (*ruach*), the wind of life. This wind of life, this life-giving power of God, is the Spirit which enabled people to come out of Egypt, resurrected Christ from death and started the church as a liberative community. We also experience the life-giving Spirit of God in our people's struggle for liberation, their cry for life and the beauty and gift of nature" (The Theme, p. 40).

Both affirmations raise the question of criteria for the discernment of the Spirit. How do we recognize the Holy Spirit among other spirits? The Assembly acknowledged that "not every spirit is of the Holy Spirit. The primary criterion for discerning the Holy Spirit is that the Holy Spirit is the Spirit of Christ; it points to the cross and resurrection and witnesses to the Lordship of Christ. The fruits of the Spirit, among them love, joy and peace, offer another criterion to be applied (Galatians 5:22). We believe that these criteria should also operate when we encounter the profound spirituality of other religions" (Section IV, p. 117). Our criterion for discerning the Spirit is Jesus Christ because we do not know any other Spirit but the one that was revealed through the manifestation of God in

Christ. This is the main centre of theological reference of the ecumenical movement.

The ecological challenge of today lends urgency to the Assembly's call for the development of a theology of creation. But it would be wrong to imagine that as Christians we could develop such a theology on a neutral or common ground with other religions or worldviews. The Spirit at work in creation is the same Spirit that was manifested in the incarnation of Jesus Christ and his ministry and came forcefully into the life of the early community at Pentecost. To open up a pneumatological reflection on creation, a more trinitarian theological perspective on our historical engagement, is not to depart from Christology, but to expand it and discern better its cosmic historical significance.

As Canberra said, "The Bible reminds us that the redemptive work of Jesus Christ was renewal not only of human life, but of the whole cosmos. Thus we have hope that the covenant promises for the earth's wholeness can find fulfillment. In Christ, 'the creation itself will be set free from its bondage to decay and will obtain the freedom of the glory of the children of God' (Romans 8:21). In the whole of the Christian life, we take up the created things of this world and offer them to God for sanctification and transfiguration so that they might manifest the kingdom, where God's will is done and the creation glorifies God forever. The sacraments of Christian worship use the elements of the created world to manifest the Triune God present among and in us. This sacramental Christian perspective influences our approach to the creation in general. We must never forget that 'the earth is the Lord's and all that is in it, the world, and those who live in it' (Psalm 24:1)" (Section I, p. 57).

The awareness of the Spirit's presence in historical movements in the world is enlivened when, in response to that presence, we participate with others in the attempt to serve the Spirit's liberating purposes. In actual obedience to Jesus Christ, we are driven to stand side by side with others who reveal in their lives the actions of the same Spirit. This discernment of the presence of the Spirit is not something theoretical; it is an existential exercise in obedience.

When we developed the covenants on Justice, Peace and the Integrity of Creation, we called on all people of whatever persuasion to rally together to support those fundamental commitments to human survival. From the Christian perspective, we affirm that in the action of the others we recognize the same Spirit of God that was manifested in Christ and in the life of the church, calling all to work for the reconciliation of all things. Of particular importance in the ecumenical experience has been walking together with the poor, the racially oppressed, the penitent, the powerless. They have helped us to understand different dimensions of the gospel and gain a more profound perception of the presence of the Spirit of God.

The conviction of the presence of uncreated energies, of the action of the Holy Spirit awakening and calling nature and history to renewal, brings with it an evangelistic occasion. The Spirit of truth uncovers and reveals all truth. As we participate in the search for a new respect for nature and a new care for our neighbour, we point to God's boundless care for creation and humanity, which was fully manifested in Jesus Christ. As humanity confronts basic questions of value, meaning, purpose and priority, to announce the creative activity of the Spirit is to point to a deeper dimension of reality and to be obliged to give account of the hope that is in us. As Father Rosato has written, "The universal search for economic and political justice stimulates Christians not only to give public witness to their own justification by faith and baptism, but also to point to the being and mission of the Holy Spirit as the source and goal of all ethical ideals, and as their mysterious and fruitful inner force" (*The Ecumenical Review*, 41, 3, 1989, p. 394).

As we see the Spirit of Christ in the cross and resurrection breaking all human barriers and announcing the kingdom that is coming, we perceive the struggle for justice in the world as a spiritual struggle. The Spirit points to Jesus Christ as the full historical manifestation of redeeming love, creating energy and consoling presence. Canberra pointed to "an urgent need for a new type of mission, not into foreign lands but into 'foreign' structures. By this term we mean economic, social and political structures which do not at all conform to Christian moral standards" (Section I, p. 66). On those frontiers, through dialogue and cooperation with others, evangelism continues to be what Philip Potter has described as "the test of the ecumenical movement".

The Spirit sanctifies

We believe that the Holy Spirit brings hope even amidst all that seems to militate against hope, and gives strength to resolve the conflicts which divide human communities. Repentance must begin with ourselves, for even in this Assembly we have become aware of our own failures in understanding, sensitivity and love. As we commit ourselves to continuing repentance, so we call all people to share in that commitment and to pray for the renewing power of the Holy Spirit to renew in us, personally and corporately, the image of God (Assembly Message, p. 3).

Most ecumenical theological conversations take the personal dimension of faith for granted and turn to discussing its consequences and fruits. Similarly, we seldom discuss ecclesial life or church growth: we assume the existence of the church, and our concern is with its faithfulness. The conciliar process for Justice, Peace and the Integrity of Creation was perhaps the first organized attempt to bridge this gap between the presuppositions of our faith and its actual manifestation in historical activities. The conciliar process and the acts of covenanting were intended precisely to take us back to a reflection on the term *conciliar*, on our covenanting status, on our identity as church of Jesus Christ. The Spirit manifested in the struggle for justice, peace and creation is the same Spirit that is calling the church to unity and to internal renewal.

So far the debate has been inconclusive. We have not yet been able to articulate together clearly the linkage of our historical commitments to the vision of the kingdom to our being the people of the Spirit, the body of Christ. But Canberra, with its main theme a prayer to the Holy Spirit, obliged us to become very personal and to testify to the action of the Holy Spirit in the transformation of persons, church and world. In the New Testament, the Spirit is sent upon the whole community and upon each one of the members of that community. The Spirit creates koinonia, community with a purpose, to call all things to conversion and reconciliation in Jesus Christ; but within that koinonia, the Spirit grants specific gifts for the building up of the body of Christ.

To be possessed by the Spirit of God means internal, personal freedom produced by the action of that same Spirit. "The Holy Spirit is gloriously free and unbound (John 3), freeing and unbinding God's people from the structures and strictures of this world (Romans 12). The challenge to God's people is to discover, accept and live in this freedom. To live in the Holy Spirit is to yield one's life to God, to take spiritual risks; in short, to live by faith" (Section IV, p. 112). This freedom is the freedom to love and to serve. It is the enabling of people to look beyond themselves to the love that God manifested to every creature and to make a commitment to be part of that all-embracing love.

This personal transformation, this awareness of the action of the Spirit for sanctification, takes place within the life of the Christian community, which is itself being submitted to the Spirit's sanctifying activity and thus freed for service to God in the world. The activity of the Spirit signifies a continuous process of transformation of the community and each of its members. The Spirit also works in the search for unity and reconciliation which is becoming more and more visible in the life of our churches.

"As the churches move towards each other on the ecumenical pilgrimage, the Holy Spirit calls us to repentance and engagement in a process of forgiveness. Churches have anathematized each other, and have contributed to polarization, leading some to define themselves in opposition to others. The churches need to repent of their stances and actions in respect to each other, and to take responsibility for the positions which they adopt and for their theologies. Without repentance and forgiveness no new creation as reconciled communities can emerge. The Holy Spirit has been evident in enabling the churches to repent, forgive, reconcile their histories and come to union in God through Christ" (Section IV, p. 115). This process of conversion, repentance, healing, sanctification, growth in the Spirit, building of koinonia, sharing in worship and liturgical celebration, and joyful recognition of the action of the Spirit in sustaining and transforming creation provides a continuous process of transfiguration.

Our ecclesiology should be rightly understood in the total trinitarian economy, reflecting the model of communion that prevails in the Trinity, and especially related to the action of the Holy Spirit in history. It needs to provide a home for all the gifts that God has granted to all members of the body of Christ. Such an ecclesiology will recognize itself as a *pars pro toto*, as a priestly community interceding for the whole.

The work of the Holy Spirit in every person, the experience of spirituality, is an entry point into the total dynamic of God's action. Our personal transformation and family reconciliation, our koinonia in the local church, our living in unity in relation to other expressions of the same koinonia and our longing for the reconciliation of all things in Jesus Christ belong together.

Canberra said in this connection that "the prayers of the worshipping community join the voice of the voiceless. Both repentance and thanksgiving are expressed also on behalf of those who are absent.

Bread and wine and water brought before God with thanksgiving represent all creation. The sharing of peace at the eucharist commits the community to work for peace. The partaking of communion symbolizes justice and love. Our dependence on the fruits of the earth for our physical and spiritual life makes every eucharistic celebration a call to preserve the integrity of creation. Through all this the Spirit keeps flowing, renewing the face of the earth. . . The Holy Spirit challenges God's people to holy living, personally and corporately. Personal sanctification and corporate transformation belong together. At all times life is to be lived under and by the power of the Spirit. This may become most manifest at times of tragedy, loss or joy in personal and corporate life" (Section IV, p. 119).

This continuous process of transfiguration, this ecclesiology of koinonia at the service of God's purpose to save and reconcile all in Christ, should become the dominant vision of the ecumenical movement, challenging our false dichotomies. How sad is our separation of personal piety from the life of the church and from God's care for creation. How narrow and sectarian is our perception of the whole dynamic of God when we do not recognize in the total ministry of the church the particular vocation of monks or nuns or people who devote their lives to contemplation and prayer for the sake of the whole. How narrow is our ecclesiology when it centres on *my* salvation, forgetting the symbolic and sacramental service to be rendered to the whole of creation. But also how shallow is our social involvement when it misses the personal dimension of sanctification and eternal life and the communal ecclesial dimension of our faith.

In all programmes of the World Council of Churches, this continuity of the Spirit transforming all reality into the kingdom to come is present. All our programmes should perceive themselves as entry points to highlight, to amplify, to dramatize and to proclaim the total economy of the triune God. In setting priorities and goals, in identifying points needing urgent attention and in allocating resources of staff and funds to serve the ecumenical movement, we must discern as best as we can where the Spirit is blowing freshly in our midst, and ensure that the work of the World Council of Churches responds fully to these promptings. Having prayed for the Spirit to come and renew the whole creation, we should expect the Spirit to renew the life of the World Council of Churches.

As we seek to be prompted by the fresh winds of the Spirit to shape the future of the ecumenical movement, let us keep in our hearts and minds this prayer from the Seventh Assembly:

"Come, Holy Spirit,
Come, teacher of the humble, judge of the arrogant.
Come, hope of the poor, refreshment of the weary. . .
rescuer of the shipwrecked.
Come, most splendid adornment of all living beings,
the sole salvation of all who are mortal.
Come, Holy Spirit, have mercy on us,
imbue our lowliness with your power.
Meet our weakness with the fullness of your grace.
Come, Holy Spirit — Renew the Whole Creation"
(Assembly Message, pp. 3f.).

III

Evangelism:
Ecumenical Frontiers Today

One of the roots of contemporary ecumenism is found in the nineteenth-century missionary movements which led to the World Missionary Conference in Edinburgh in 1910. Out of this and other manifestations of God's Spirit, among both Protestants and Orthodox, a calling to unity developed which found its biblical reference point and inspiration in the prayer of our Lord "that they all may be one, that the world may believe" (John 17:21).

The WCC Basis is itself a statement of the gospel message: "The World Council of Churches is a fellowship of churches which confess the Lord Jesus Christ as God and Saviour according to the scriptures and therefore seek to fulfill together their common calling to the glory of the one God, Father, Son and Holy Spirit." To true ecumenism belongs the awareness of being part of the missionary movement of God's own self, who, in the fullness of time, sent the Son to redeem us and sent the Holy Spirit to gather together a people to be the bearers of the revelation of God's liberating will in Jesus Christ.

It is with joy that the World Council of Churches assumes its responsibility for reminding the churches of our common evangelistic calling. This function has been addressed in a wide variety of ways during the history of the WCC, especially since its merger in 1961 with the International Missionary Council. The responsibility for witness and support for common witness in each place cannot be confined to one department, but must be a matter for fervent prayer and concern in all aspects of the Council's life, an integral part of all aspects of its work. Just as the unity of the church is essential to our participation in the struggle for justice in the light of God's promise of reconciliation in Jesus Christ, so the proclamation of justice and an attitude of service on our part are a testimony to the common faith in Jesus Christ which has brought us together in the ecumenical family.

In the 1960s Faith and Order conducted an important study on "The Finality of Jesus Christ in an Age of Universal History". It discussed the radical novelty of the person of Jesus Christ in the context of a cultural situation in which the various national and regional histories and the corresponding diversity of cultural forms were beginning to come together, pressing us to accept the relative nature of our particular convictions.

Today the challenge is perhaps even greater, since we have to speak the name of Jesus and show the newness of life offered in him in a world where the vision of global reality is measured in billions of years and genetic manipulation can condition life itself. In such a world, the announcement that the ultimately new came at a given time and in a given person is a greater surprise and scandal than ever before.

There is something ingenuous about affirming that God was in Christ reconciling the world to God's own self. There is something childlike about pointing to the child of Bethlehem, to the one who was condemned on the cross, as the symbol and centre of a radical transformation of the human condition and of the whole of the universe itself. Yet it is in this story with its ingenuousness and childlikeness that we find the freshness of mind we need to confront the great contemporary perceptions and to testify to a reality that illuminates them and calls for their creative transformation.

In what follows I will suggest three important aspects of the contemporary context in which the churches are called to witness together and to undertake, with the WCC's support, "their worldwide evangelistic and missionary task", as the WCC Constitution phrases it.

The nature of humanity

The prevalent mood of our day seems to be a pragmatism whose highest norm is a constant increase in productivity and competitiveness. On the one hand, by shaking up the dogmatic certainties of yesterday, this new pragmatism opens up the possibility of a far-reaching debate on the human being and on the human calling and destiny. On the other hand, it invites us simply to go along with the drive for increased productivity and consumption as though the human being could be reduced to an economic variable.

The classical socialist schema understood human alienation as a result of oppressive social structures, and postulated that human liberation would come through a revolutionary change of those structures and collective ownership of private property. Creative work, underpinned by forms of social organization based on solidarity, would constitute a secure basis on which to build a new human being and a new society. This perspective was complemented by a progressive view of history, which called for present generations to sacrifice for the benefit of those to come.

Philosophically and in practice, all such dogmatism has virtually collapsed today. The roots of alienation go deeper than the structures of society. Although the Christian word "sin" is seldom if ever used, there is general recognition of the corruption of power and the bureaucratic inertia which displaced creativity as the motor of society. The self-realization of the new human being is not automatic but needs to draw on human values recognized by the community, and demands social mechanisms of democratic participation to control and inspire new structures of human relations.

This new social dynamism and desire for participation in political, cultural and economic life calls for Christian witness at various levels — first of all by making a contribution to society through a Christian presence which embodies the values of the gospel. The dimension of personal diakonia is now highly appreciated in societies which once thought that the problem of solidarity had been solved in structural terms but have now discovered the need for dedication, commitment and a personal touch to bring gospel values into the daily life of the community.

At another level, the new situation demands that Christians, and theologians in particular, take part in national public debates to determine essential values. Tradition, emotion, beauty, creativity, freedom, but also the ideas of guilt and responsibility, of forgiveness and new beginning, of newness of life and freedom — all these are elements to be witnessed to in dialogue, providing a new opportunity to express the gospel message in terms which challenge accepted ideas and invite people to look with fresh eyes at the person of Jesus of Nazareth.

The contemporary debate on the nature of humanity is by no means limited to the socialist and formerly socialist countries. In the West today we find practically universal acceptance of the philosophy of the Enlightenment, which has culminated in a secular pragmatism and consumerism in which the product is truth, religion has become privatized and market competitiveness has become the idol to which everything is sacrificed. It has been fascinating to follow the debate in the European Community in its attempts to create a Europe without frontiers. It proved relatively easy to establish a society with free circulation of capital; it is more difficult to guarantee the free movement of people. But most difficult of all will be the building of a social Europe given that, in the prevailing thought, social costs are regarded as a burden damaging to international competitiveness.

Whether in serving and caring for the victims of these economic developments, or, at a deeper level, engaging in the theological-ideological debate and upholding human values in contemporary technological society, the churches have a new opportunity to speak the name of Jesus Christ and point to him as the man for others, the one who took upon himself the fate of the outcast, who proclaimed forgiveness and spoke of eternity — the one who proclaimed the new year of the Lord, the new and free possibilities of God.

The WCC's conciliar process for Justice, Peace and the Integrity of Creation is not only, or even essentially, an ethical convention, an agreement on what must be done in the organization of society. It is first and foremost the affirmation of a new relationship between human beings and the creation, a new covenant of responsibility between present and future generations. In short, it is a new way of proclaiming the gospel message, pointing towards Jesus Christ as the one in whom the forces of destruction have been condemned, bridges of reconciliation built and the full dignity of the life of every human being and the integrity of creation affirmed.

The presence of Christians practising liberating diakonia in the life of society and proclaiming the gospel as they participate in society's search for new models is a concrete announcement of good news. All our ethical reflection and social action must be done in constant lively dialogue and interchange between real situations and the gospel history, expressed in theological insights which open up the radiant perspective of the eternal, the "numinous", the new. In responses, the World Council of Churches should increase its capacity to relate to the widest possible diversity of churches in local situations, so that we can create the necessary links to enable the churches to benefit from and contribute to similar experiences elsewhere in the world.

Science and technology

A fascinating new frontier for evangelism is opened up by current developments in biotechnology. The important thing to remember in this debate is never to lose sight of two dimensions which cannot be separated: pure research and its possible consequences on the one hand, and economic power on the other.

At stake here is not only the potential of science for good and evil, but something more: the definition of humanity, the affirmation or denial of human freedom and integrity, the possibility of a transcendent relationship with the mystery of God — which is in fact denied in the more extreme potential expressions of biotechnology, which bring us close to the demise of freedom in the definition of the human.

This is not an entirely new theme for the World Council of Churches. It was raised by the World Conference on "Faith, Science and the Future" in 1979; and it has arisen in the explorations in the Justice, Peace and the Integrity of Creation process of a theological understanding of creation which can free us from the functionalism that has led to the exploitation of nature and take us towards a more sacramental, eschatological and biblical vision of the transformation of all reality according to God's purpose of restoring all things in Christ (Colossians 1:19-20; Ephesians 1:10).

When some self-styled scientific circles reduce the definition of the human to the transmission of genetic information from generation to generation, we have a cosmic vision which is in a real sense pathetic — heroic, perhaps, but meaningless. It is not the first time in the development of science that we find ourselves on the borders of secularized materialist determinism. More than once in the past the sum of the available data has led some people to visualize the world as a closed circuit devoid of reference to external values or internal spiritual realities. On the basis of our faith that in Jesus Christ God has acted to reveal the meaning of creation and our affirmation of freedom of choice, integrity and human responsibility, we are clearly on a collision course with the extreme claims of certain contemporary expressions of science and technology. This is a philosophical debate of the first order: the encounter between the idea of a genetic chain reaction and hazard, chance as the cause of mutations, and purpose as a cultural element intervening in the chain but from outside it.

Theologically, the affirmation of a spiritual dimension can sometimes be accommodated with the data known to contemporary science, but at other times it has to be held in dialectic contradiction because it seems impossible to arrive at a new *Summa Theologica*. In other words, we cannot simply resign ourselves to accepting an essential dichotomy between natural knowledge and the knowledge given by the revelation. But neither can we make knowledge of the natural world the limit of revelation. Thus, the proclamation of the good news and God's liberating will in Jesus Christ will assert ethical demands for justice and respect for human dignity in any process of scientific investigation and technological application. But this good news will inevitably find itself in a dialectic dialogue with the worldviews implicit in much of contemporary scientific and technological effort.

On the one hand, in the light of the good news of the gospel, we affirm that enquiry into and investigation of the creation is a human right and duty. In so doing we affirm the rationality and cognizability of the real world. We understand it as making us better able to read the mind of God. On the other hand, we constantly proclaim the human values which all scientific and technological research must serve. In so doing, we urge the need for research to make us better able to worship God with all our mind, with the intelligence of our being, but at the same time we call for discipline in research so that it may be done with a sense of service to personal life, loving interpersonal relations in the building of human society and preservation of creation's integrity.

Paradoxically, the intentionality of research, which is largely initiated, directed and controlled by the economically powerful, affirms the importance of options, priorities and purpose in understanding reality. Yet in the face of the obvious relationship between market or political forces, technological developments and scientific research, we cannot fail to put forward other values and affirmations about purpose, freedom, integrity and justice — values which cannot be explained by the content of research as such, but by the ideal of humanity, the vision of a spirituality in whose service we would like to see the whole intellectual process of humanity.

Culture as the bearer of transmissible knowledge, tradition (especially church tradition) as the training ground of conscience and above all the history of Jesus Christ in the gospel summoning us in love and commitment to the service of others — these are things which can and should be analyzed scientifically, but with a perspective which recognizes an historical dynamic that is constantly changing and innovating and cannot be reduced to any form of determinism.

Our evangelizing concern here is not confined to questions of ethics. Rather, we hope that Christians in the world of research will join with us to identify the real questions and to begin to formulate a few faltering responses to them.

But if the evangelizing word may come to us from those directly involved with the questions, possibilities and uncertainties of the laboratory, it will also come from the people who, far from the laboratories, feel in their own lives the aggressive impact of technology which they cannot influence or control. It is the meek of the earth who will remind us that responsibility and power cannot be reduced to laboratory coordinates, but are urgent questions that require us to take sides in the struggle for justice, ethical values and solidarity. The meek of the earth have Jesus Christ as the standard-bearer of humanity who promises fullness of life and solidarity. We cannot proclaim the good news in the world of science nor expect the expressions of technology to affirm it unless the dimension of justice — the demand for humanity raised by the humble of the earth — remains fundamental in determining the scientific, technological and intellectual options of our community.

To proclaim the gospel of Jesus Christ is to speak a name which rings strangely in the world of genes and mutations and phenomena evolving over billions of years. But the name of Jesus Christ speaks of an historical action in which human sin and aggressiveness are not simply accepted as destiny or as the limits of the human condition, but are actively assumed as a responsibility, as guilt, and find response within history in his redemptive death on the cross. The new life which is offered in Jesus Christ is a process of sanctification, opening the way for the transformation of the whole of reality as a purpose intrinsically present in the creative energies of creation, and as a vocational project to which all human beings — including scientists — are called. The advent of biotechnology calls the churches to re-examine the fundamental Christian understandings of the creation and the relationship between God, humanity and the created world. To give a foundation for this address to the challenges of biotechnology, the resources of the biblical witness and the declaration of the ancient creeds — which begin by affirming faith in God as the Creator and Maker of heaven and earth, of all things visible and invisible — must be reaffirmed afresh.

If the gospel of love is to permeate all human relations, it is absolutely essential that our ecumenical structures maintain a living link between the scholars and the meek of the earth, between the wisdom of the humble and scientific research. The affirmation of new life in Christ and of the dimension of spirituality in the middle of a genetic chain which seemed to be affected by chance but is now subject to the influence of technological power, is an evangelizing vocation that challenges us and calls for our cooperative effort.

A world of many faiths

As we fulfill our calling to preach the gospel, we come into contact with people and organizations of other religious faiths or of no faith. Our meeting with them is witness. The missionary nature of God's message in Jesus Christ calls us to approach others in the same spirit of love, sharing and communication as ruled the life of the man from Nazareth. This mission in solidarity with others is accomplished in the Abrahamic tradition of prayer for others, illustrated by Jesus. There is a responsibility of "the part for the whole", the Christian community for the whole human community, which is also expressed in service: "As the Father sent me, so I send you". It is this same spirit of openness and concern for others that enables us to describe Jesus in his life as "the one who came to do good" and to see the cross not simply as the manifestation of human evil, but fundamentally and above all as total giving of self for the liberation and redemption of others.

The subject of our attitudes to one another is more urgent than ever before in view of the almost simultaneous awakening in all the world's major religions to an awareness of their own identity and, in many cases, of their own missionary responsibility. Our quest for dialogue with other faiths is dominated by the need for harmonious co-existence — the need to build total human community. We have only to read the daily press to see the proliferation of ethnic conflicts with a strong religious content, in which fanaticism plays a destructive role that makes it more difficult to witness to spiritual values among people estranged from all religious feeling. The work of evangelism demands searching together with members of other faiths for a *modus vivendi*, a way of organizing society which will provide a degree of freedom in which all of us are at liberty to "convince and be convinced". We are all too quick to recognize the fanaticism displayed by adherents of other religions, forgetting the sombre pages of our own Christian history and forgetting that sin, in the form of sectarian pride, always lies in wait for us as a potential enemy.

Our relations with other faiths are not just a matter of the co-existence or even "pro-existence" of the different religious groups. What is involved is also an attitude of dialogue, an attitude of respect for the neighbour in keeping with that shown by God in Jesus Christ. Consequently, our testimony to our faith should take place in a context not only of respect but of acceptance of the other. Jesus does not hesitate to point to the Samaritan as setting the example of love for his Jewish disciples. In Christ God offers God's self. God does not impose. The outstretched arms of the cross are perhaps the best symbol of God's attitude towards all humankind — the offering of God's self in an attitude of total powerlessness, and from the depths of despair appealing, inviting to a free decision. The witness we owe to the other is the witness to God's love made manifest in Jesus Christ — a love to which I can testify only in a loving relationship which implies acceptance of my neighbour and co-responsibility for the whole human predicament.

Our reflection and encounter with people of other faiths have led us to ask ourselves a more personal question: What have I learned about my own Christian faith from the faith of others? We are invited to examine our own convictions in the wider frame of reference of the convictions of others. The questions which thus arise oblige us to re-examine our own faith in depth and to express it in terms which make sense not just for us but for others.

In no way does this process of examination affirm that the gospel of Jesus Christ is to be found in other religions. Although there have been interesting studies of religious typologies which have sought to discover a common symbolism in many of humankind's religious expressions, it is not in this direction that our concern for under-standing our faith in relation to the faith of others leads. Rather, we are called to allow ourselves to be challenged by others and to try, in the spirit of the cross, to explain in words and deeds the reality of a love which seeks to embrace all of us equally.

There is a third level to this ecumenical debate: the old yet ever new question of the theological value to be recognized in non-Christian religious experience. The problem has to do not only with our relations with people of other faiths but also with the whole significance of religious or philosophical movements within the uni-versal perspective of the Christian faith. Various answers have been put forward on the question, which I shall not go into further here. I have been helped by careful study of Romans 9-11, where Paul takes up the problem of his own people's unbelief and at the same time opens up the eschatological dimension through which it would be possible to understand how, in God's mercy, what we regard as "hardening" could have had a positive function in the overall context of human history.

But none of the three levels of our ecumenical experience in the matter of the role and place of other faiths questions the central tenet of our faith: that God was in Christ reconciling the world to God's own self. The spirit of dialogue, friendship and encounter with my neighbour provides the ideal context for witness. To accept the questions addressed to us by other religious faiths is to adopt the attitude urged by Peter: "Always be prepared to make a defence to anyone who calls you to account for the hope that is in you." And in trying to evaluate the role of other religious faiths in God's eschatological plan, let us remember that when the Apostle Paul affirms his faith and hope in an eschatological understanding of the role attributed to Israel after the coming of Christ, he does so not as an excuse for not bearing witness to his people, but out of passionate concern that they should all come to know Jesus (Romans 9:1-3; 10:1). The missionary conviction of the Christian faith is not called into question, but rather is purified, strengthened and deepened when we place ourselves alongside our neighbours of other faiths in an attitude of respect, of listening and appreciation of the cultural and spiritual treasures belonging to them.

Too often when Christians articulate the central motivation for evangelism, the basic attitudes required for mission, we allow ourselves to be guided by a negative judgement of the other instead of by contemplation of the crucified Christ and his loving service. Theologically it is clear that the gospel is by definition for others, but it is so as the expression and message of a non-sectarian love. We rob our neighbour if we fail to evangelize, we rob the gospel if we indulge in proselytism. We serve the gospel by loving one another, by listening, by living together in harmony, by working to overcome barriers.

We must look in greater depth into the subject of what kind of social, political and legal organization could provide a constructive framework for harmonious coexistence among the religions. We shall have to equip ourselves to relate to religious groups and organizations, including churches, in quite specific situations where interreligious tension seems to be reaching a breaking point. How are we to relate to organized religion in places where political power plays a role, where there is conflict, and where the theological question is more difficult because it comes in terms of power relations, social organization, ancestral prejudices? The good news of the gospel, which speaks to us of God in Christ breaking down all the barriers that separate human beings, is our constant source of hope even in situations where fanaticism — our own and that of others — seems to bar the paths to reconciliation.

* * *

Evangelism is fundamental to the ecumenical calling and to the *raison d'être* of the World Council of Churches. Our clarity in confessing Jesus Christ as God and Saviour and calling others to faith and Christian discipleship is the guarantee of our Christian authenticity and our ecumenical work. This dimension of proclamation can be lived out in practice in the encounter with the great debates of the contemporary world, the fundamental questions raised by scientific and technological efforts, and in our relations with men and women, organizations and movements who proclaim other faiths or worldviews.

Participation in the whole of human life, in a spirit of dialogue, tackling the power factors which condition research and technology and seeking to build responsible societies, is a pragmatic necessity, but even more it is a fundamental requirement of the gospel which points towards the incarnation of God in Jesus Christ. This is the only valid theological method for evangelism: conscious participation in the whole of human life and its problems. When all is said and done, for the great mass of the people, evangelism is not a question of apologetics but of life. Gustavo Gutiérrez once said that in Latin America the people are "poor and believing". Much the same could be said of the vast deprived masses of the world as a whole.

Our challenge is to explain the faith in terms of joy, faithfulness, justice and solidarity. We are called to bear witness to the God of justice, hope, consolation and reconciliation, seeking to identify with the poor and the marginal. Like John the Baptist, the ecumenical movement points towards the crucified and risen Christ: "Behold the Lamb of God, who takes away the sin of the world!" (John 1:29), and with the Apostle Paul we proclaim him as "the power of God and the wisdom of God" (1 Corinthians 1:24).

IV

Missionary Identity
and Interfaith Dialogue

Friends of other religious persuasions sometimes complain that Christian missionary activities are insulting. They would like to see self-restraint on our part — or even some legal protection — to prevent what they see as attacks on their convictions. While we regret and repent of past and present mistakes in how Christians have borne witness to Jesus Christ, the missionary dimension of the Christian faith is intrinsic to it. It cannot be eliminated without affecting the reality of that faith.

I would compare our situation to that of Jewish friends who demand that their allegiance to the state of Israel be considered as an essential part of their being Jewish. They do not defend every activity of the state of Israel, but they claim that their faith has an intrinsic relationship with this land which cannot be eliminated without affecting its very nature. This position is polemical, often disturbing, but clear. It would be easier, perhaps, to dialogue only with Jews who are willing to take a distance from the historical existence of the state of Israel. But genuine dialogue with a community needs to address the issues that are central to its self-consciousness.

Missionary identity

It is my contention that in the encounter with people of other religious persuasions or no religious persuasion, Christians should confess openly their missionary identity. It belongs to the centre of our faith, to our understanding of God. It is basic to our Christology and to our anthropology. God is love, consuming love for creation and creature; and the whole of creation should be conceived as the visible manifestation of that love of God which communicates existence and life. The Spirit of God is affirmed as the sustaining life-giving reality. We recognize God's communicative, sustaining nature in all the stories of the Bible, but fully in Jesus Christ — the redeeming, reconciling, suffering, liberating God calling all human beings to partnership and communion. This awareness of God's own nature, which is the secret source of all human creativity, is for Christians the foundation of their testimony.

This missionary responsibility is present even in the Old Testament. The election of the people of Israel was understood as being for the sake of all humankind. Abraham was to be a blessing to all nations. Jerusalem was to attract the people of the world as the "city of peace". This missionary conviction was not an invitation to personal conversion but the proclamation of a destiny with implications for the whole world. So it was natural for the Jewish writers of the New Testament to proclaim that the events which had taken place in Jerusalem and Judea and Samaria had a universal significance. In the long history of the Christian church the awareness has been maintained that the event of Jesus Christ has consequences for the whole of humankind.

The central conviction of the Christian faith is the incarnation of God in Jesus Christ. This decisive event is fully related to every historical event and conflict and at the same time points to a quality of life that breaks the chain of events and opens the window to eternity itself. The affirmation of this faith in the creed is the contention that we have here a revelation of God's own self which constitutes a powerful invitation to rearrange our life, our priorities, our commitments. If Christians believe so highly of Jesus Christ, how could they keep such news for themselves? If the whole universe and the life of every culture and every human being are ontologically affected by God's manifestation of reconciling love in Jesus, how could such good news be reserved for Christians only?

The question of who is Jesus Christ is always open for discussion in the light of historical, scientific and literary research. In the encounter of Christianity with different cultures over the centuries, different images, symbols and understandings of Jesus Christ have emerged. The contemporary reopening of this question attracts me very much, because in the perspective of the struggle for liberation of the poor people of Latin America we are discerning new shapes of the figure of Jesus Christ. Surely the living encounters with people of other faiths will project new angles of vision and perspectives of depth on our understanding of Jesus Christ. But if in order to have a fruitful dialogue, one must redefine the central conviction of one's religious community, then it is an exercise in mutual deception and futility.

In academic discussions, for the sake of the argument, we sometimes try to remain "neutral" or "objective" in considering the evidence concerning the existence or nature of God or the meaning of life. It soon becomes evident that such presumed neutrality is no more than an honest attempt, and that it is impossible to forget the reality of our Christian identity. After "going secular" in our philosophical and dialogical approach, we discover that our fundamental convictions and images and values reappear at the end of our search in a way that indicates they were always there. It will be far better in a living encounter with ideas and people of other convictions to recognize our identity as our point of departure.

Take for example the whole notion of God. At the end of the day it is almost impossible for people coming from the Christian tradition to arrive at figures, images or propositions concerning ultimate reality that depart from the vision of God we have received in Jesus Christ. When we consider nature as revelation or natural law as our guide, we come to conclusions that accommodate natural law to convictions that have been cherished long ago in the Christian family, obviously rooted in a consideration of God's revelation in Jesus Christ. As in the Old Testament we need to understand the exodus in order intelligently to read the story of creation, so also after the death and resurrection of Jesus Christ we cannot look to any aspects of reality independently from that central event. It will help both us and our partners if we put that reality clearly on the table of our dialogical encounters.

There are situations today in which the delicate political balance of power or even the law of the land makes impossible an open centrifugal or even centripetal kind of mission, where conversion is prohibited. In such circumstances, the Christian identity is preserved by intercessory prayer on behalf of the whole nation and the whole world as part of the worshipping life of the Christian community, being a church for others, carrying on a priestly role on behalf of humanity.

Even more, the missionary nature of the Christian faith is rooted in the life of prayer of the Christian community. When we pray "Our Father who art in heaven", we cannot conceive this Father as the tribal head of one particular group of human beings. This prayer taught by Jesus affirms the family nature of humanity's relation to its

Creator. It affirms the caring attitude of God to the whole of reality. It invites us to look for the kindgom to come, to enter into the dynamic of constructing a human society of fraternity and love. Our prayer brings into our consciousness the eschatological dimension that will embrace the whole of humanity. It is impossible to pray to the Lord Jesus and then to limit it to a particular sector of humanity that we call Christianity.

The dimension of priestly responsibility for the whole inhabited earth is present every time the eucharist is celebrated. Even if no "evangelistic invitation" is extended and no proclamation to the outer world is involved, the very being of the Christian community is built around the notion of a world called to redemption in Jesus Christ, for which the church is fully responsible.

This missionary dimension is also present in the normal participation of Christians in the life of society. I should not try to impose on others my religious perspectives or values, but I cannot refrain from testifying to my closest convictions and submitting them — and their fruits — to the scrutiny of others. At the same time I must be ready to receive exactly the same kind of contribution and similar demands for correction from other religious and ideological convictions.

Even in pluralistic democracies, growth is needed in this area of respect for the other's identities and convictions. For centuries Christians in the West have claimed the right to send missionaries and to establish churches within all cultural groups. But neither the laws nor the patterns of behaviour in Western societies are yet able to accommodate honestly the convictions and needs of people of other religious persuasions. It is imperialistic to use parliamentary law to impose canon law, whether the canon is Christian, Muslim or Jewish. But it is nonsensical to prevent the open discussion of perspectives that have flourished within our different religious communities. To ignore our identity in our contribution to the total well-being of our society is to make the society poorer, weakening the quality of the debate and postponing today's problems until tomorrow.

Our Christian missionary identity is also based on a certain anthropological conviction. The nature of a human being is a "sent nature", a missionary one, a vocational one. Both religious teaching and ideological systems call our attention to the *homo faber*, to the capacity of human beings to transform creation, to create new realities and to advance civilizations and cultures in the process of building up human society. From a Christian perspective all human beings are called to be co-workers with God in the administration of creation, in the proclamation of liberation and in the affirmation of a new human reality, a day of peace that is God's promise for God's creatures. This biblical vision involves a missionary vocation. Every person is called to be, to do, to participate as one fully responsible to God and fully responsible for human fellow beings.

This "sending" nature of the human being is perhaps the central contribution of Christianity and other religions to the search for a participatory democracy. No one can be only an object of the decisions of others; all are called to be fully responsible for their personal destiny and the destiny of society as a whole. To be for others means to be at the service of others, but also to share our best with them — and that means sharing the central conviction of our life. There is an element of justice to this: how could we preserve for ourselves something we consider of supreme value for our life and for the life of the whole of humankind?

But does this insistence on our own identity and central convictions involve an attitude of superiority in relation to other religions? Knowing the past record of Christian attitudes in relation to people of other religions, seeing many of the conflict situations of the world today and recognizing our own paternalistic tendencies in relation to our neighbours, we cannot make light of this danger. Yet at the same time we should recognize that in Christian theology and in our actual relations with people of other faiths there are safeguards against it.

The first of these is the sense of amazement that we can have a knowledge of God in Jesus Christ, which belongs to our Christian identity. We do not believe that any particular merit or wisdom or moral virtue of our own has enabled us to come to this knowledge. It is precisely a concentration on the person of Jesus Christ which opens our eyes most clearly to our shortcomings and sins. The cross which stands at the centre of our Christian conviction is a rebuke to all human pretensions and should be a protection against all manifestations of superiority.

Second, we recognize that being a Christian is very often the consequence of a geographical accident. We were born in a place where the Christian tradition prevailed or where people of Christian persuasion came, but millions of others around us could not even consider becoming Christian because they were born in entirely different circumstances and under other influences.

Third, we cannot look to the history of the missionary expansion of the church without seeing the horrors committed in the name our missionary conviction. A sober analysis of this history works as a corrective to all neo-colonialist missionary practices. But if this is still ignored, as is unhappily the case with many new sectarian manifestations of missionary practice, let us hope that ecumenical debate and actual encounters with people of other religious convictions will help to overcome this denial of the very gospel that they want to announce.

The gospels open our eyes when they point out that it was among people from outside Israel that Jesus found the best manifestations of faith. We are invited to discover and affirm the reality of beauty, of suffering, of love, of commitment to justice that exist outside the so-called Christian boundaries. There is no way for Christians to claim a monopoly on human or even Christian virtue. On the contrary, we are invited time and again to thank God for the cultural and religious achievement of people of other faiths.

A fascinating theological discussion is going on within the Christian family around the reopening of the old debate about the word *filioque* in the Nicene Creed. Does the Spirit proceed from the Father *and the Son* (*filioque*), or only from the Father? Behind the historical polemics around this question lies the great debate about how we perceive the actions of the Spirit of God outside the historical Christ and beyond the realm of the Christian church. The Spirit who was active in the creation of all things continues to be present in the human creativity manifested in society, in cultures, in religions. While the Spirit is the same Spirit of Christ, and it is not possible to discern contradictory activities in the being of God, the Spirit has a realm of action which Christians are invited to discover in the light of their experience of Jesus Christ. Our faith invites us to expect manifestations of the Spirit of God in all creation. More and more we are led to discover with amazement that God is not the prisoner of the Christian church but has witnesses in all nations.

The debate for truth should continue, and conflicting claims will be present in our dialogical encounters. This debate belongs to the very nature of bringing forward our respective identities. But it means that, from a Christian perspective, we cannot be proud of our Christian achievements because all of them are pure grace; on the contrary, we have reasons to repent of our shortcomings and to come humbly to the encounter with people of other convictions. In these encounters we are made aware of the manifestation of what for us are Christ-like values, which indicate the action and the presence of the Spirit of God.

Contemporary Christian theological discussion has helped us to discern new dimensions of Christian truth when we look at the gospel stories through the eyes of the poor, the marginalized, the women. In inter-religious dialogue, too, we are helped also to look back into the meaning of the biblical text and into the richness of our tradition through the questions, testimonies and challenges of people of other convictions.

This is not a spirit of superiority or a judgemental attitude to others; it is simply that the experience of Jesus Christ has made such an impact on our minds and hearts that we are impelled to share with people who, through historical circumstances or decisions of their own, are not yet able to attach such an importance to the historical events of Palestine in the first century of our era.

Pointing towards Jesus is our only specific contribution to the total life of humankind. We are aware that others will have their contributions to offer. We do not expect a kind of general syncretism, but we expect reciprocal knowledge that will help us to understand and to accept each other. We expect the development of a climate of relationship in which everyone has the right to convince and to be convinced. We work towards the development of an interreligious relation that will eliminate the reciprocal caricatures and the real danger of using our emotional religious loyalties as divisive elements in human conflicts. In such a permanent dialogue we can bring from our respective traditions the best contributions to enable humankind to overcome tensions and to affirm a new day of justice.

The elements of dialogue

But this of course gives importance to the discussion of the "rules of the game". How do we relate to each other? How do we encounter each other? What factors need to be taken into consideration in our interreligious encounters in the light of our experience and the diversity of situations in the world?

1. First, in every dialogical situation the relations of power between the participants should be taken into consideration. Dialogue does not happen in a void; it is not an intellectual exercise behind the protected walls of a Western university. Dialogue is very often a matter of life and death. It is carried on in the middle of

tensions that divide human communities, at both the level of options to be considered and of emotions that are being raised.

One sometimes hears the church's present emphasis on dialogue with other religions contrasted to its attitude during centuries of colonization by the European powers. The suggestion is that Christians today are interested in dialogue because they no longer have the power to impose their convictions on other people. Unfair as this accusation may be, it has enough historical points of reference to oblige us to think of the sincerity of our attempt and to recognize that the acknowledgement of past and present power relations with our partners is a fundamental condition of the possibility of a creative dialogue.

In certain regions representatives of the majority religion are not interested in dialogue with minority groups because merely sitting around the table with them in organized dialogue would provide a "recognition" they are unwilling to grant. In other circumstances, a minority religious group has been able, because of the colonial history, to educate its members and constitute an elite in the society; they have, if not the power of numbers, the power of institutions, of education, of hospitals, and so on. In those conditions the invitation to dialogue is perceived by people from the majority religion who have less social power as being a manipulative attempt to proselytize. There is no easy way to overcome these situations. Much will depend on personal relations, reciprocal knowledge and the openness to consider the objective factors of division in society.

Even more difficult are situations in which religious cleavages are synonymous with social, political and national loyalties. Consider, for example, the situation of Israel, Jerusalem and the Occupied Territories. While it is possible to develop a very fruitful and intelligent dialogue between Christians of Western origin and Jews of Western origin, dialogue between Arab Christians and Jews who have migrated to Israel from Muslim countries is practically nonexistent. We also recognize the difficulty of direct dialogue between Islam and Judaism, which is fundamental to that situation. The power relations are such that people cannot perceive the possibility of a encounter as equals. To quote an Arab Christian, "When I know that the other has a machine gun at home to be sure that I keep quiet, how can I carry on a dialogue with him?"

Unless we are ready to keep open the lines of communication and take the risk of looking to the future, there is no way to overcome this kind of painful situation. Of course, there is a danger of being used, of being "softened", of allowing lofty consideration of interreligious relations to disarm one's militancy and sense of belonging to one's people. One also risks being misinterpreted by members of one's own religious or ethnic group. Thus, it is absolutely necessary to involve a community of prayer and support, a community of trust, in order to protect ourselves from the temptation to seduction and at the same time to be able to explain to our own communities the motivations and values of opening to the others.

An illustration of the influence of the power factor comes from the encounter of Christianity and Marxism, which, though not a religion, is an ideology that sometimes assumes the forms of a religious creed. In Latin America the theology of liberation has been able to use Marxist instruments in the analysis of society and to maintain an ongoing dialogue with representatives of the Marxist philosophy and ideology. Such contacts did not happen in countries with a socialist-Marxist government. When both liberation Christianity and Marxist political movements are under persecution, it is possible for the two to enter into dialogue, to cooperate and to create coalitions. But when Marxism was the ruling power in Eastern Europe, dialogue relations were limited to common agreements on questions of peace. Very rarely was there a dialogue in which the very ideas and convictions of the partners were on the discussion table.

While the ideal situation for a dialogue is that in which neither partner is afraid of the other, this ideal does not always prevail. Yet because dialogue is absolutely necessary, risks should be taken to promote it. Why? This leads us to our second consideration.

2. Much present-day religious dialogue seems to originate in the affirmation of rational discourse and a tolerant attitude towards others that is accompanied by a certain relativism of convictions. If we do not believe that anybody can come to final philosophical truth, we can invite everyone to express his or her own convictions in the hope that all will learn in the process without having to pass judgement and without being threatened.

Some modern Christian attempts to interpret the reality of the plurality of religions from a supposedly neutral ground — nature or creation or an idea of God unrelated to revelation in Jesus Christ — betray this search for an "objective" perspective from which all religions could be justified and dialogue is understood as the logical expression of the relation between different roads to the same goal.

But what happens if someone does *not* share this philosophical presupposition? What happens with those Christians who want to be in dialogue with people of other faiths but who insist that Jesus Christ is the crowning of all the aspirations of humankind? Could we develop a dialogue starting from different theological or philosophical presuppositions?

My contention is that the dialogical attitude should not be bound to a specific philosophical presupposition, least of all to a relativist one. Dialogue should be an encounter of loyalties, in which the question of reciprocal identity is fundamental. Dialogue, respect and openness to the other should be so anchored in our own religious conviction as to be an integral part of the central core of our confession. Dialogue needs to be rooted in the centre of one's own faith precisely in order to confront the kinds of historical difficulties that we have mentioned. We are obliged to be open to our neighbours of other faiths notwithstanding the danger of being politically weakened or misunderstood.

It is important to develop within our religious communities a theological-ideological reflection so that the members will understand, from the very centre of their faith, this need to be in relation with others. From a Christian perspective, the other cannot be considered as a "target" for Christianity or as a non-entity, but as one in the encounter with whom something of a foretaste of the encounter with God takes place. Only as we anchor the value of dialogue in the central convictions of our faith are we able to eliminate the elitist character of our dialogue and multiply the normal and joyful encounter of all members of all religious communities.

Others might offer different rationales for dialogue. We must recognize that some of our internal reasons for encountering our neighbours may not be acceptable to people of other religious persuasions. A serious school of Christian theology considers as "anonymous Christians" all those people of other religious convictions who do not confess Jesus Christ, but whose lives indicate the kind of decisions that would make them excellent Christians if they had a chance to know Jesus Christ. I doubt that many friends of other religious persuasions would appreciate this name: they would like to be considered in terms of their own set of values and their own faith loyalty. But we can find something similar in other religions. When some Muslim friends picture Judaism as the primary school, Christianity as the secondary school and Islam as the university, and invite us implicitly to go forward to graduation; or when some Hindu friends consider adding Jesus Christ to the pantheon of divinities through which it is possible to progress in our spiritual pilgrimage, I am not happy either. But the important thing is that from within our respective convictions we discover ways to affirm our relation to the neighbour and the openness to give and take.

3. While the normal dialogical situation is bilateral, involving people of two different religious persuasions living side by side and coming together to share experiences and concerns, multi-religious dialogue is growing. Though multilateral dialogues may have a certain artificiality because the problems remain so general, they do fulfill several important roles.

For example, it is relatively easy for Christians and Jews to engage in dialogue and in cooperation. Of course, there is the long history of Christian harassment of the Jewish community which cannot be ignored; and after the "holocaust" it is impossible to start a conversation as if we were just beginning. But in general terms, after a recognition of that history, it is possible to walk together because of the common treasury of the Old Testament and because of a similar reading of reality in terms of prophetic historical conviction. A multilateral dialogue in which Christians and Jews are in the company of Muslims, Buddhists, Hindus and others enlarges the conversation, avoids easy solutions to our differences, reminds us of the rights and needs of others, and brings the challenge of mystical religions to our prophetic perspective.

From a Muslim point of view, it is easier to have a relation with the "People of the Book" — Jews and Christians — who share a certain notion of revelation. A multi-religious dialogue will remind all participants of the existence and rights of others and in this way oblige us to expand our initial perspective. Bilateral dialogue — Muslim-Christian, Muslim-Jewish — grows beyond its limited character when challenged and enriched by the presence of entirely different traditions.

Multilateral dialogue is also necessary to avoid fixing lines of agreements and differences between religions on ideological or ethnic grounds rather than on religious perspectives. Very often history has produced a symbiosis between a particular ethnic group and a particular religious tradition. The encounter is an encounter not only of religious loyalties, but also of ethnic, cultural loyalties, making more difficult the possibility of religions to overcome ethnic-racial boundaries in the pursuit of both truth and a constructive living and working together.

In Sri Lanka, for example, a multilateral dialogue could go beyond the distinction between Sinhalese and Tamils. While the majority of Sinhalese are Buddhist and the majority of Tamils are Hindu, there are enough Christians and Muslims in these two ethnic groups to provide at least the possibility for religious encounters which bring people of the two groups to a religious dimension of loyalty and mutual correction. Under the circumstances of ethnic tensions and war the pluralist religious dialogue provides a platform from which to look at the conflicts of society which, though not providing magic solutions, offers a new meeting point for people who, if they were to respond only to their ethnic motivation, would remain far apart.

Finally, multilateral dialogue can affirm and defend certain common values as a contribution to the whole of society — for example, religious freedom. This is important not only for regions in which a particular religion is dominant, but also for situations where secular governments and ideologies prevail, with some initial prejudice against religion or without much knowledge of religious conviction. In general, peace, disarmament, confidence-building and cooperation in international reconciliation are central to multilateral dialogues; and indeed it is in this area that most of the initiatives for multilateral dialogues have found a fruitful soil. But it is also possible to encourage and develop multilateral dialogue in terms of more limited local or regional needs, transforming different religious loyalties into common projects for the development of a whole village, of a whole region.

A particular temptation to avoid is the mobilization of religious forces against the rest of society: to create a religious front either for protection or to impose certain "religious" values. Precisely out of the awareness of diversity within the religious world we become aware of the wider diversity among people of no religious convictions or of different philosophical outlooks. The concern of multilateral dialogue and cooperation is not to affirm particular rights for religious people, but to help society as a whole to develop legal and cultural norms that will help people of different convictions to live together, united in the common project of building up the nation and the community.

4. Interreligious dialogue is a value in itself and should be recognized as a vocation within our different religious communities, just as

in the Christian community we recognize certain persons whose main vocation is diaconal service and others who have a particular gift of rendering testimony of their faith. Interreligious encounter does not need to be justified in terms of other values but has a validity in itself. At least two components of dialogue should be highlighted within that specific vocation:

• *Reciprocal testimony to the basic convictions of each of the partners.* Growing in the knowledge of our traditions, cultures and values and learning from each other is fundamental. The questions and answers that belong to a dialogical situation oblige the participants to raise soul-searching questions about their own identity that will help each to better self-understanding and to clarify their own positions. The other, coming from an entirely different perspective, functions as a mirror reflecting my image, my reality, as an invitation to repentance and to change.

The consideration of the communities to which we belong, with their shadows and lights, with their various attitudes in relation to people of other convictions, cannot be absent from a dialogical situation. Not only our goodwill and reciprocal personal disposition is at stake; it is an encounter with different worldviews, different histories, different social realities. This encounter of reciprocal commitments necessarily produces moments of difficulties, tension and passion, but this is a necessary path into growth both in our self-understanding and the understanding of the other and in the sharing of our most cherished values.

Witness is a normal component of every in-depth dialogical situation. As the WCC *Guidelines on Dialogue* state, "We do not see dialogue and the giving of witness as standing in any contradiction to one another. Indeed, as Christians enter dialogue with their commitment to Jesus Christ, time and again the relationship of dialogue gives opportunity for authentic witness."

• *Care for the building up of the total society.* Religious establishments are not called to replace the structures which society has organized to tackle social, economic and political problems. Normally the collaboration of people of different faiths in the search for solutions to those problems will be organized through those political structures not necessarily related, or even better not related at all, to our religions and allegiances. But it is a fact, as the WCC *Guidelines* say, that "common activities and experiences are the most fruitful setting for dialogue on issues of faith, ideology and action. It is in the search for a just community of humankind that Christians and their neighbours will be able to help each other break out of cultural, educational, political and social isolation in order to realize a more participatory society."

Many political structures follow ethnic or religious lines. A religious dialogue can help to overcome sectarian approaches and to point beyond our respective party-lines to the welfare of the whole community. Religious people may come together because they are concerned with the same society; they may also come out of their respective religious conviction. To care for the totality of the society encourages the participation of religious-minded people in their search for better solutions for the whole of society.

The great challenges of peace, justice and ecology are very clear invitations to the common search for solutions. But we must be very much aware that all these questions have the potential of becoming religiously partisan. We must be sure that the dialogue around those issues helps to inspire the participation in the search for justice or to make the necessary separation of religious passion from the search for common and secular solutions to community problems. In every case the practical response could be different, but the availability of a platform for religious dialogue will help to find the necessary degree of intelligent participation from a religious perspective and with religious passion on the different issues of society.

5. It is necessary to speak very briefly on the question of religious syncretism. Many are afraid of entering into dialogue because they think that behind it lies a hidden or open attempt to produce one "world religion" by mixing different components of our respective traditions. As far as I know, no religion is interested in a kind of basic world religion and even less in a religion whose identity lies in its pretension to express the future world religion. Syncretism as a project is totally artificial. Religions respond to historical developments and have created different cultures, different perspectives. They have a life and value of their own, and no one can bring them together into a single pattern.

Of course, every religion has its own interpretation of the existence of the others, and within every religion we can find several interpretations, sometimes conflicting, of the value and significance of the others. More and more in Christian circles there is a theological and eschatological affirmation of the validity of other religions, held together with the affirmation of the specific vocation of the Christian church for the whole world. It is a dialectic consideration that affirms the missionary identity of the Christian faith, its witnessing stance, its responsibility for the world and at the same time recognizes that God did not remain without witnesses and that the wonders of his creativity are visible in people of other religious convictions. This tension between the two affirmations allows and even demands a dialogical attitude towards the neighbour without the pursuit of syncretistic solutions to the multiplicity of religious convictions.

Of course, in a dialogical situation we live side by side, and thus there are many opportunities for encounter and recognition of the best of our respective traditions. It is unavoidable that some reciprocal penetration takes place. We might talk of cultural syncretism. Christians hope that this will be a Christ-centred syncretism. Others will look at it from a different perspective. But we will not be closed to the possibilities of reciprocal influence that exist in our dialogical encounter, even to the risk of conversion.

In the long centuries of church history we have different models of encounter of the story of Jesus Christ with the different cultures of the day: Jewish, Hellenistic, Latin, German, and today Asian, Latin American, African and so on. We are learning also to develop the expression of our Christian faith by responding to the aspirations of women, racially discriminated groups, the poor, the marginalized. Unavoidably, our religious life is being shaped by the encounter with others.

Syncretism is not a goal; it is not something to be sought. On the contrary, a dialogical situation allows for the affirmation of our respective identities. At the same time, only God is in control of the future, and only the Spirit knows the dimension of truth that God will open in front of us.

V

Ecumenical Social Responsibility

One of the constitutional functions of the World Council of Churches is "to express the common concern of the churches in the service of human need, the breaking down of barriers between people, and the promotion of one human family in justice and peace". Indeed, for many people this function — the affirmation of justice and peace — is the most visible image of the Council. Some would go so far as to say that we have almost reduced the gospel to its horizontal expression, social service.

Those who know the WCC from within are aware that this is not so: that worship and biblical studies play a fundamental role, that concern for the unity of the church is a constant theme, that the proclamation of the gospel is affirmed as the privilege and responsibility of every Christian, and that the service in society we do offer is not a secular activity but an affirmation of our basic Christian convictions.

The unity of humanity is not a fine ideal in the clouds; it is part and parcel of God's own revelation. Here if anywhere the vertical dimension is essential for any action on the horizontal plane. Likewise, the aim of the whole emphasis on Justice, Peace and the Integrity of Creation (JPIC) is both a conciliar process manifesting the unity of the church and an evangelizing proclamation of the will of God in Jesus Christ to liberate.

These three dimensions of the WCC — unity, witness and justice — are intimately linked together and must be understood as points of access to the whole dynamic of our ecumenical calling, never as separate compartments which do not interpenetrate each other.

The life of the Council has brought a wealth of practical experience in expressing the concern of the churches to serve human need — emergency work with refugees, calling the people to organize for their liberty, prophetic proclamation of God's judgement on history, action in solidarity with those struggling to transform situations of oppression.

In the independence of Namibia, in the coming of democracy to Chile, in the rapid changes which have taken place in Central and Eastern Europe, the ecumenical movement has been present, playing a humble but necessary part. It is the people, the popular movements and the churches who have been the primary agents involved in these events. The supporting work of the ecumenical movement and especially of the World Council of Churches is there to be analyzed and criticized but it is undoubtedly significant evidence of the enthusiasm with which the attempt has been made to fulfill its constitutional role by action which expresses the churches' concern in serving human need.

In what follows I will highlight three contemporary challenges to the ecumenical movement as it seeks to live out the concern for service in the face of human need.

Models of society

The changes in Central and Eastern Europe have set in sharp relief the question of what type of society we are seeking to build. These countries have clearly rejected the prevailing authoritarianism and expressed the desire to be integrated in the mechanisms which are dominant in the economy of the world market. Many in the West have welcomed this desire to accept the market economy as a triumph of the capitalist system as a whole. But the question society has to consider also confronts those Third World nations which have tried capitalist models for development without managing to emerge from their situation of marginalization vis-à-vis the great world centres. In this new departure in world history the hope is that a fresh debate will open up, both locally and globally, in the quest for possible alternatives.

To the outside observer the WCC seems generally able to frame global eschatological visions, proclaim the peace of God and describe the horrors of the prevailing realities but to have difficulties in clearly propounding what have been called "middle axioms", ways by which to approximate to actual political commitments and realities. While there is recognition that the World Council of Churches fulfills a prophetic role, it is sometimes faulted for contributing very little to the practical choices facing men and women, particularly those in positions of authority in society.

"Utopia" as a mobilizing concept is absolutely necessary. The theology of liberation in its various expressions has shown us how it can mobilize oppressed peoples, calling them to create symbols of hope and to be the agents of their own history. These peoples are beginning to see that God's promise is a direct challenge to the existing situation.

But this eschatological, utopian vision needs to be supplemented and sustained by studies and practical activities which show how within history we may come closer within history to the coming kingdom. Perhaps we have to resume the studies begun in the 1970s on a "Just, Participatory and Sustainable Society". The theme was not taken to its conclusion. After the debate in the Central Committee in 1979, in which we could not find an approach to dialogue and understanding between different theological interpretations of the dynamic of history, we lost sight of the theme and it was watered down. To some extent it has reappeared in the conciliar process for Justice, Peace and the Integrity of Creation, but the specific search for models of society was left on one side. Today as we receive the fruits of the conciliar process and read the contemporary historical situation, we are challenged to define images of society which can help those who have to take urgent existential decisions.

In JPIC we have learned that the three key concepts of justice, peace and creation form an integral whole and must always be considered in their inter-relationship. So, too, the idea of a just society along the lines of the jubilee, of justification, of rehabilitation of the neighbour, will have to be explored together with the idea of sustainability, of what is possible and what is productive. The idea of sustainability has to be governed by the idea of justice and of mechanisms for support and solidarity in building up the weakest sectors of society. Participation, understood in terms of representative democratic policies, structures of joint managership and voluntary forms of social service must be thought of in terms of contributions to the sustainability of society as a whole. We are looking for a society worth sustaining because of the quality of its life.

The quest for a new model of society involves not only analyzing ideas but also assessing experiences of cooperativism, of people's organizations whose struggles for definite objectives help to build a solidarity that may serve to support more general visions for the reorganization of society as a whole. We need a mobilizing vision and possible historical approaches. An intellectual effort is necessary to identify, describe and explain our roots in the gospel, our use of the Bible and Christian tradition, our methodologies for approaching actual historical situations and our reasons for the choices we make.

As the World Council of Churches we cannot and must not end up with a programmatic blueprint. That is properly the task of each specific society and of the society of nations as a whole. But through critical service of what is there and through support for the experiments of community solidarity existing in the four corners of the earth, we can and must appeal for, motivate and equip participation in the political sectors of civil society.

In the reflective work of the WCC there will always be a certain untidiness, a lack of definition and coherence, since the Council by its very nature is a meeting point for different experiences and approaches, and the persons and situations are always changing. But the value of the ecumenical contribution lies in this very untidiness, because we accept the dialogue of cultures and systems, we acknowledge the right to divergence and we are mutually critical as we listen to each other and answer each other and seek to overcome our respective limitations.

But while we are looking for this model of society, which is absolutely necessary and in the quest for which the WCC will be able to play a useful role and offer a truly global framework, we must always remember that the starting point of our reflection and our action is a warm concern for actual human beings — the children, the marginalized, the oppressed. Our history has given us experience on the frontiers of the struggles for human rights, for racial justice, for the dignity of woman, for the recognition of the poor as the agents of their own history. The freedom, creativity and responsibility which are the marks of human existence from a Christian point of view do not allow us to accept deterministic ideas of history which marginalize or destroy the weakest members of society in the name of the god we call "the market" or the god we call "class".

We offer these values from our gospel faith to the contemporary debate, not as virtues on which Christians have a monopoly but as contributions to a quest that goes beyond the boundaries of Christianity. This discussion must develop in the setting of vigorous cooperation and dialogue with people of other faiths and ideologies. The values we formulate must be communicated to the rest of the community in categories that are acceptable in multifaith, multicultural dialogue. It is necessary and appropriate for us to do our own work within our churches to explain the convictions arising out of the encounter between our faith and the realities of society. But we cannot do this work in isolation, without taking into account the presence of other value systems and other religious views of the cosmos whose protagonists also want to contribute to this debate. A great challenge is the creation of societies which are sensitive to the values and freedom of each of these views of the cosmos and at the same time can state common convictions, thus making fruitful and creative coexistence possible. Much work remains to be done to affirm liberty fully in a responsible society.

The importance of diakonia

Diakonia, understood as a gift of the Holy Spirit and as a manifestation of practical love for human beings who are in need, has been and remains a substantive element in Christian existence and in the life of the church. Justin Martyr, writing in the year 150, goes into detail about the strong linkage between the sacrament (the mystery) of the Word, the sacrament of the altar (the Lord's table) and the sacrament of our brothers and sisters:

> The day called Sun-day an assembly is held in one place and the records of the apostles or writings of the prophets are read for as long as time allows. Then the president in a discourse admonishes and exhorts [us] to imitate these good things. Then we all stand up together and offer prayers: and bread and wine and water are brought up and the president likewise offers prayers and thanksgivings, and the people assent, saying the Amen; and there is a distribution, and everyone participates in [the elements] over which thanks have been given; and they are sent through the deacons to those who are not present and the wealthy who so desire give what they wish, as each chooses; and what is collected is deposited with the president. He helps orphans and widows, and those who through sickness or any other cause are in need, and those in prison, and strangers sojourning among us; in a word, he takes care of all those who are in need.

This spirit and practice of service has been present in different forms through the centuries. From its beginning, the World Council of Churches has been faithful and constant in fulfilling its call to serve basic human needs. Yet one sometimes gets the impression that this diaconal work does not receive the recognition and consideration it merits. The "glamour" lies in other dimensions of our work. I would like to think that we are freeing ourselves from more or less negative attitudes towards a primary diakonia which meets the visible needs of the neighbour, but we still have a long way to go. Compare for instance the difficulty in getting funds for an old people's home with the relative ease in finding money for what we call "development" projects or for those projects which hold out the promise of total liberation.

There are reasons which can explain but cannot justify the second-class status diakonia seems to have in major ecumenical discussions and in daily life. First of all, the "cup of cold water" is clearly no substitute for the wells we must dig. Diakonia may seem to be dealing only with the symptoms and not with the causes of the problem. So it would seem right to concentrate our efforts and resources on structural transformations of society which would overcome the social problems which challenge us today.

In the second place, we have developed a theology of service in which society as a whole and government in particular are responsible for the education, health and well-being of all. Where the state does not or cannot provide the necessary services, the church has offered them. But as soon as the state can assume responsibility for these, it is thought that the church's direct responsibility has ceased. There has been little sympathy in ecumenical circles for the view that the state has the responsibility for only those services which private institutions, including the church, are not capable of offering. The prevailing ecumenical mood puts the emphasis on a responsible society in solidarity, in which basic human problems are faced together by society and not simply delegated to the enterprise of vocational sectors.

Although these two reasons help us to understand the problem, they can in no way justify contempt for an activity which, besides being constitutive of our identity as the church, is increasingly necessary in today's world. New situations oblige us to overcome the opposition between service and development, diakonia and liberation, by making it more and more evident that direct immediate social service helps towards credibility and the development of liberating practices which tackle all the problems of society.

The tragic earthquake which struck Armenia towards the end of 1988 called forth worldwide ecumenical solidarity to help Christians, the church and the whole people to build and rebuild, to deploy all available forces in coping with immediate human needs and planning reconstruction of social life. The ecumenical presence met a real need and aimed only at diakonia. However, the physical earthquake, tragic as it was, did not represent the major challenge for the Armenian people. Their very survival as a people and as a religious and cultural entity is at stake in the dramatic moments of their history today. While the ecumenical presence was conceived in response to practical needs, reconstruction clearly has a great deal to do with the moral fabric of a people, its capacity for resistance and the affirmation of its own history, faith and culture in the future. As an ecumenical movement we cannot see the global political solution to the problems which have arisen among the nationalities of the former Soviet Union, but we do know that our practical aid to overcome the consequences of a tragic earthquake contributes to the creation of a climate of faith in the future, of international solidarity which inevitably has consequences in the way the global problems of this society and those around it are faced.

Repeated famines in the Horn of Africa have called for solidarity on the spot to make it possible to save millions of lives. The work is neither "liberating" nor "revolutionary"; it is the distribution of basic foods to enable people to live for another day or week or year. The repetition of these phenomena and the devastating civil wars in Sudan, Ethiopia and Somalia are an invitation to despair that all our efforts are vain and futile. But it is the churches' participation in serving the immediate need which gives moral authority and the capacity to take part in the great national debates which are needed to achieve a constructive and lasting peace.

Perhaps the best example of interaction between diakonia as a response to immediate human need and the struggles for wholesale liberation of a people is given by the Special Fund to Combat Racism. The vast majority of the projects approved and financed by this Fund have been projects answering to very specific human needs: seed, medicines, books, clinics, refugees. In other words, while the "glamour" of the people's movements is in their struggle for liberation, the concern of the WCC has been to cooperate with them in those immediate responses to human need which should not and cannot wait for the success of the people's struggle for liberation. But the underlying significance of the Fund's contribution to these basic services is not confined to this. It connotes moral and even political recognition for the movements. In the first years of the Special Fund, international polemics, especially in the countries of the North Atlantic, concentrated on the recognition of these liberation movements implicit in this aid through diakonia. The WCC is not ashamed to aid those aspects of the struggle which some would consider secondary. Yet this has been the vehicle which expressed moral support, the recognition of the authenticity of these movements as genuine representatives of large sectors of the people in their respective countries.

Discussions within the WCC have led to a better understanding of the dynamics of international aid in terms of service and the sharing of resources. Three dimensions of this are of special concern today.

The first is the need to reaffirm our calling to diakonia and to multiply our efforts in relation to the demands of our faith and the new situations we face in the world. With our Orthodox brothers and sisters we say that "faith in Christ without a diaconal mission loses its meaning. To be Christian means to copy Christ and to be ready to serve him in the person of the weak, the hungry, the downtrodden and, in general, the person of those in need. All other efforts to see Christ as a real presence, without coming into contact with the needy, are nothing more than pure theory" (from the third Pan-Orthodox Pre-Conciliar Conference, 1986, quoted in *The Ecumenical Review*, 40, 2, April 1988, p. 171). This basic conviction must urgently be made plain today in service in those countries which thought they had found an answer to the fundamental needs of personal and family security and are asking now for help from the civil society, especially from the churches, to meet emergencies arising from the economic difficulties they face.

But beyond these changes, linked to moments of swift social change, the growth in world population — reaching dizzying heights in the Third World — raises problems in two areas:

● Abandoned children: There are millions of children in large cities who live on charity, household refuse and often prostitution and delinquency. While many cathedrals close, thousands of children huddle together and cling to each other trying to give each other a little warmth to survive another day. The efforts of UNICEF to combat infant mortality and call attention to this fundamental frontier of human dignity must call forth the best endeavours of the churches and make us open to imaginative participation.

● Older people: There is a growing number of people in the "third age" sector, losing the physical strength to work and needing greater care if they are to survive. Industrialization and urbanization throughout the world have destroyed the traditional bonds of support between the generations. Alternative forms of care must be discovered to dignify the last years of life for large sectors of the population.

The great danger that some minorities in the world may not survive till the hour when freedom comes also requires a multiplication of our diaconal efforts. Especially in Latin America we are concerned for the survival of the indigenous communities. While we struggle for recognition of their rights to the land, to their history and dignity, there is an immediate, parallel task which makes that struggle authentic, and that is to contribute to their mere survival.

Second, our concern is not only to increase our efforts but also to affirm their spiritual dimension. No doubt we as churches can support the effort of many others to respond to disasters and emergencies. But it is also certain that on the basis of the fundamental affirmations of our faith — God in Christ making the human situation his own, Jesus Christ putting children at the centre of his concern — we have a spiritual approach which must be present both in our actions and as a leavening agent in society.

We must anchor our aid in our faith in God's redeeming, liberating purpose, so that we can resist and persist in situations which seem to repeat themselves without any promise of a solution — not only great natural tragedies like desertification, but also great transnational economic processes which continue to widen the gap between the "haves" and the "have nots".

Resistance, perseverance, endurance in aid will be possible in so far as we trust in a providence with resources beyond what human wisdom enables us to visualize. The act of loving is an act of faith in God's resources. It is an affirmation of hope, an invitation to a new beginning.

The spiritual basis of our diakonia must also bring a personalizing dimension into all our work. Just as God in Christ invites us to a personal decision and calls us by our own name, so Christian social aid has to be seen in terms of persons with whom we serve in the name of a common dignity and a common hope. There are huge problems which have to be confronted with solutions on the largest scale. But time and again, where there are personal relations, not only material gestures are communicated but also the profound spiritual symbolism of a human presence alongside another human being.

A third and particularly important dimension of service today is that connected with the role of the community, the Christian congregation in diaconal service to the whole of society. In no way must diakonia be thought of first and foremost in terms of international aid. Rather, diakonia is the presence and development in every Christian group of its possibilities of mutual aid and community service.

One of the undesired effects of the multiplication of international missionary aid and service relations has been the creation of symptoms of dependence on this international aid. Much of the work of churches in impoverished countries depends almost entirely on financial contributions from churches and fraternal organizations in distant countries. This approach is understandable in view of the deteriorating economic relations in the world, but it brings with it growing dependence on imported models of service and social action which require professionals. There are local, traditional styles of aid which logically must be rethought and brought up to date to deal with new situations, but which still have a great deal to contribute.

Churches in industrialized countries have tended to delegate their diaconal work to professionals. While this approach has enabled the service given to be scientifically effective, it has deprived that service of human warmth and the sense of community and endangered the spiritual values of the personal approach and of rehabilitation.

A genuine ecumenical debate on diakonia is needed, which would involve the churches in economically wealthy countries, in order to define clearly this dimension of community participation in social service as a requirement of the gospel and an indispensable contribution, given the growing depersonalization of our societies. Such a dialogue in depth would help us to define the diakonia appropriate for society as a whole, which must be a prophetic demand of the church and part and parcel of our Christian identity. At the same time it would enable us to invite other faiths and other sectors of society to enter into a debate to which we are all committed.

The basic theme of aid to the neighbour in need must be discussed as a mutual challenge and as an element which can forge relations of mutual trust. The debate will not be easy because it will be necessary to recognize the existence of a variety of theological and ideological presuppositions in ourselves and in others. Relations with other faiths are becoming a fundamental priority for all ecumenical reflection. I mention it here in the context of diakonia; earlier it was in relation to the quest for models of society; in considering a third aspect of our theme, too, the service of peace, we shall have to reintroduce the importance of interfaith encounter and cooperation.

Promoting peace and justice

The ministry of reconciliation — "breaking down barriers between people and the promotion of one human family in justice and peace" — has been central to the ecumenical movement from its very beginnings. During World War II, the World Council of Churches in Process of Formation organized meetings between Christians from Nazi Germany and the allies with a view to exploring ways to peace. The conversations were very practical and a variety of possible solutions were considered. There was no agreement — a useful reminder to us that we are not always successful in our efforts! But it is important to remember that even in the midst of an ideological division as fundamental as that which existed during World War II, the ecumenical pioneers knew they had to try to build bridges for peace and then reconciliation.

The Amsterdam Assembly was deeply concerned with the disorder in human affairs in a world which must conform to God's order, confirming the call for reconciliation and the responsibility of the WCC to explore avenues for overcoming the Cold War. That the Assembly in 1948 did not find it appropriate to say anything about the conflict which directly confronted the government of the Netherlands with the patriotic forces of Indonesia struggling for decolonization is a reminder of our historical oversights and the consequent need for avoiding triumphalism when we think of our successes in this area.

While the WCC is not able to be pacifist in the sense of totally rejecting violence, as in the tradition of some of our member churches and of the Fellowship of Reconciliation, it has never, with the sole exception of the Korean war, approved military intervention as a means of solving national or international conflicts. Systematically it has rejected war as a solution to conflicts and affirmed peace and dialogue as approaches to reconciliation, which is always possible. This experience of almost fifty years has taught us some lessons which we must reaffirm today.

First of all, we have learned that peace can never be achieved by sacrificing justice. The work of diplomacy makes sense when it is placed in the service of the people to defend their rights and meet their most pressing needs. In my first press conference after being elected WCC general secretary, a journalist asked me whether because of my known pacifism I was going to change anything in the Programme to Combat Racism. Implicit in the question was a caricature of PCR as an activity which supports violent action. I answered that the only change I could imagine would be to strengthen that work considerably, because I knew of no better service for peace in the WCC than that rendered by PCR in its support for the claims of the humble and above all in its condemnation of racial discrimination as violent action exercised against the people.

Because we are concerned to have a peace founded on justice, we have to arm ourselves with endurance until our attitude is understood and we can play a role — humble or significant — in the achievement of peace. For example, the WCC has always been very clear in its affirmation both of the right of Israel to exist and the rights of the Palestinian people to have their own homeland. Many groups representing the Palestinians or the Israelis are concerned by that stance. But we are certain that sooner or later our position will be understood as stemming from a demand for justice which cannot be left to the side in the ultimate resolution of this problem. "Righteousness and peace will kiss each other," says the hopeful promise of Psalm 85:10. This is the fundamental inspiration guiding the work of the World Council of Churches in this passionate quest for peace, which recognizes no other way than the way of justice.

Second, we have learned that the global impact of the WCC in any situation determines the effectiveness of the Council's activity in helping to solve the problems in that region. In Africa, the WCC's longstanding support for the process of decolonization, its diaconal aid to meet basic necessities and assist in the formation and education of "middle managers", its militant participation in acknowledging the legitimacy of the struggle for the liberty of the colonized peoples, its holding up of the spiritual dimension through appeals for prayer, ensuring priestly intercession for the aspirations of oppressed peoples — all these, plus the political support represented by declarations, representations, boycotts is known and appreciated. As a result, we have an opportunity and invitation to more active participation in solving national or international conflicts in Africa. The total impact of the World Council of Churches creates the conditions that make the work of peace-making in dialogue possible, credible and necessary.

In some situations the different sectors taking part in a struggle prompt intervention by the World Council of Churches to help in the peace processes. Usually these stories cannot be told until much later because of the delicate nature of the work the WCC undertakes. At the same time we have to recognize that the overall image projected by the WCC has often closed our access to the sectors with power in Western countries. But we cannot seek that access if the condition is giving up our calling for justice. If we had to choose between solidarity with the oppressed peoples of the Third World and access to the sectors of power it is clear where our choices would lie. Yet we must recognize that discussion and dialogue with the great industrial and financial centres of today's world are necessary if we want to be of use to the peoples who are suffering from the injustices of international processes. We must encourage dialogue with Christians within power structures who want to live out their own Christian faith honestly, without illusions, recognizing the structural constraints from which we all suffer, but hoping that fellowship in the faith may open up new possibilities which we previously failed to see.

A third lesson is that this service of peace entails close cooperation with national churches. It is essential — and sometimes it is the most important contribution we can make to resolving conflicts — that within each nation a people of God should be formed which is aware of its responsibility for justice and peace. Mobilization of Christian people within situations of conflict will make it possible to contemplate the creation of attitudes which are receptive to initiatives that can overcome conflicts. The relation with the churches and ecumenical movements is essential because they are the real agents. When transnational corporations have wished to meet with the WCC to justify their presence in South Africa, the only thing we have been able to do is to tell them to go and make their case convincingly with the churches and people of South Africa. It is they who must indicate what the tempo and content of our support should be. The action we take is always support in solidarity, important perhaps, but always secondary.

Not that the WCC can do nothing beyond the degree of awareness or liberty shown by the local churches. That is so neither in our statutes nor in our practice. Every activity of the WCC in a specific country presupposes discussion with the national churches. But the World Council can and often must act and give its views even in opposition to the opinion of the local church. Mutual correction in solidarity is a must. We know situations where nationalism limits the vision of a church or where the prevailing fears paralyze it. There is indeed a duty to listen, so that we can then together seek to support the churches in their mission within situations which appear to be totally closed. But the aim is always justice and peace. Like every human relationship this one is full of ambiguity and exposed to error.

Beyond the particular situations of conflict between the WCC and a national church the basic principle must be affirmed that the churches' participation in countries where conflicts occur is essential to our mode of working and our being a fellowship of churches.

Today we are in a privileged situation as a World Council of Churches in the ministry of reconciliation. We have to multiply our efforts and strengthen the relational aspects of our work in order to be able to be a serious presence in so many situations of conflict or where our ecumenical conscience calls upon us to act. New areas of concern are created by the ethnic-national and religious conflicts reappearing in the countries of Eastern Europe. Here there is a special ecumenical responsiblity because many of these conflicts are encountered by Christians of different traditions, faithful to different ethnic groups, and others are in danger of confronting Christians with those who follow other faiths. While the relations between the great power blocs have entered a period of détente, local, national and international conflicts unhappily do not seem to grow less. The ministry of reconciliation must be given renewed consideration in the total perspective of the WCC. Precisely because those who pay with their lives are the meek of the earth, who are, according to our Lord Jesus Christ, the privileged object of the love of God, we must multiply our efforts to affirm our calling of reconciliation. It is not a "diplomatic" activity; it is an act of service and of obedience, which we neither can nor wish to abandon.

We are a community of love, a community of prayer which passionately seeks in reflection, action and solidarity to be useful in the quest for models of more just and humane societies, in the expression of a practical love for the neighbour today and a passionate affirmation of a peace based on justice. In whatever we do we must be sure that the hope-bringing solidarity of the World Council of Churches with those who struggle for human rights, for the dignity of women, for the affirmation of the cultural identity of peoples remains clearly at the centre of our prayers, our plans and our identity.

VI

Christian Responsibility and Refugees

The World Council of Churches, in close cooperation with its many member churches, has been involved in service to refugees since even before its own official formation in 1948. Concern for refugees and displaced persons, originally motivated by the cataclysm of World War II, is one of the sources of the very existence of the WCC. Today the WCC is charged with a task of mobilizing, coordinating and supporting the work of its member churches and ecumenical agencies on behalf of refugees.

The sense that this is one of the fundamental manifestations of Christian identity is rooted in the experience of the people of Israel as related in the Old Testament. The events that shaped the life of the Hebrew people more than any other were the experience of captivity in Egypt and their exodus to freedom. When foreigners were living among them, the reminder came again and again: "Remember, you were also foreigners in Egypt." They remembered that their fore-fathers had come to Egypt looking for protection from difficult economic conditions. They also remembered that after years in which they lived happily alongside the local population, the political condi-tions changed and they began to feel the burden of oppression. The call to freedom as expressed by Moses and followed by the people wandering through the desert of Sinai towards the Promised Land is a parable of people moving out of slavery into freedom and searching for new possibilities. This fundamental experience of oppression and liberation is at the heart of the Hebrew consciousness and remains a motivating factor in our understanding of our responsibility towards aliens, foreigners, those who are different.

Christian behaviour in relation to foreigners, especially political refugees and asylum-seekers, cannot be objective and detached. It must be a passionate commitment: those people belong to the same history of oppression and liberation that lies at the root of our consciousness. It is because we recall that we were once in the same position in which these people find themselves today, searching for protection and hope, that we put ourselves at their side, working for their liberation as in the past others have worked for our liberation.

In the New Testament this tradition is symbolically illustrated in the story of Joseph and Mary and the child Jesus being obliged to escape to protect their lives. Herod's soldiers search for the child in order to kill him, and father and mother are forced to seek protection and asylum in Egypt. There is a great symbolic meaning here. Egypt, a symbol of the oppression of the past, is now forever associated with the protection of the child Jesus. In other words, no human situation is closed forever. There is always a chance for a new opening in history, for a change from oppression to liberation, from repression to solidarity.

So whenever Christians look towards migrants or political refugees, they look to the child Jesus. Jesus says in Matthew 25 that he will be found in those little ones who are in need, those who yearn for personal care. These words come to life in reference to refugees today. Recent Christian pronouncements have emphasized God's preferential option for the poor, God's particular love for the poor, the powerless, the outcast. It is precisely the refugees of today who best symbolize the situation of powerlessness that is synonymous with the notion of the poor in the Bible. From a human perspective they have nothing to claim. They are just knocking at the door, waiting to be received, expecting a judgement to be pronounced. Those who have no power of their own are precisely the favourites in God's eyes, and for that very reason they are the centre of concern of the Christian community.

The role of the churches

The main working principle of the WCC in the service to refugees is to ensure that the protagonist's role belongs to the local churches. No centralized organization could ever provide the human support necessary in this particular service. Local churches at the national or parish level are able to provide an expression of welcome, protection and real personal interaction for people who need to feel that they are human beings, deserving of dignity, members of the human family.

The service to be rendered by local communities must begin with the prevention of the causes which produce political refugees. Churches must work for human rights in their own countries. They must try to raise before public consciousness and with the political authorities the need for the solidarity that will prevent as much as possible the creation of new waves of political refugees. But the fundamental role of local communities is to provide psychological, spiritual, personal and social support to individuals and families who arrive at their doors.

Churches are not bound so much by legal definitions of refugees as by their understanding of the mandate to express love to human beings in concrete ways. Thus, they can provide protection and support to all whose position is legally undetermined and who, although not yet officially defined as political refugees, represent equally urgent need. Local congregations and national churches have greater freedom to take action to protect individuals than international structures. The local church is able to promote aid for resettlement, to provide family support, to express an attitude of welcome to people trying to reorganize their lives in a new country. And, of course, when political refugees are able to return to their home country, the local churches there have an important role in receiving them.

The service of the churches to refugees and asylum-seekers can be seen as the natural result of an attitude of love to one's neighbour. However, because of the polemics that have come to surround protection given to refugees in many countries — with those who try to protect refugees suspected of political motivations and of organizing parallel structures of power in society — it has become necessary for the churches to articulate theologically the rationale for their work.

Churches are not alone in their service to refugees and indeed do not pretend to be the most important agency for protecting asylum-seekers and supporting refugees. There are international organizations, such as the United Nations High Commissioner for Refugees, programmes developed by states and many private organizations inspired by the most diverse philosophies. Since the churches are called to offer what they have, they contribute from their basic conviction, from their history, especially in the Western world, and from their present positions in different parts of the world. Nevertheless, the churches are in a privileged position in relation to service to refugees for several reasons:

- Churches are free from traditional definitions which classify people seeking political asylum into different categories. While we need to be aware of the definitions provided by governments and international organizations like the UNHCR, it is obvious that the overall categories of need, oppression and powerlessness are the predominant ones for the churches. In order to serve efficiently and in a cooperative way, churches will need access to the resources of the international community, and will necessarily have to make distinctions, but in no case should such distinctions constitute a straitjacket limiting the service and protection they provide.

• Churches have a transnational character, or, to put it another way, they constitute a universal reality. Most churches belong to a particular people and culture, but the common affirmations and values around which they gather are of a universal scope. They cannot defend the interests of the people of one nation against the interests of the people of other nations. To be sure, there is often a tension here between belonging to a community and wishing to serve within it and recognizing at the same time the universal dimension of the human family, which is one of the basic convictions of the Christian faith. This universal character enables the churches to contribute an important element to national discussions on refugees, because it provides them with a network of solidarity and a source of information for assessing the situation of the refugees' countries of origin and their prospects for the future, which is one of the greatest difficulties in discerning the need for political asylum. Because churches work with the people at the grassroots level, they have access to information which governments may not have.

• Churches have a central role in shaping public opinion about the application and revision of national laws concerning asylum-seekers. While churches in Western countries are no longer in the same powerful position to determine legislation as they once were, they still have a chance to raise awareness in society and to bring a perspective to the discussion which may escape legislators obliged to think of the immediate political consequence of their decisions. The entry of the churches into the public debate concerning the law and its application is a fundamental component of any progress in a more general humanitarian direction.

• Local Christian communities form a reservoir of service which has already been mobilized in many ways but has enormous potential for greater service. In order for this potential to be realized, we need to undertake a campaign of raising awareness within the churches. But, inspired by the central affirmations of the gospel, we should not find it difficult to recruit many more of our faithful in reaching out to those people arriving in our nations.

● Finally, the church, especially in the Western countries, has a tradition of providing asylum to people struggling for their lives. For centuries the churches were granted, in law or in practice, a certain role in preventing societies from exercising their power in ways ultimately detrimental to individuals. If little remains of this old tradition on the statute books and in church practice, it has not entirely disappeared from the consciousness of society. As religious bodies, churches are supposed to have an impact on the values of a given culture or society. Thus, it is logical that people in difficult situations should appeal to those values and search for the church's protection in interpreting and implementing them. Again, the church cannot pretend to be the only determinant of the consciousness of society, but it must be there, constantly reminding society of its basic values — values of both the gospel and the national traditions — lest expediency have the last word in deciding how to cope with delicate problems of human rights and human protection. Churches must incorporate a kind of final hope, a symbol of the last recourse provided by communities for those who are in desperate situations.

Church and state

Thus Christian tradition, the church's self-understanding and direct appeals from those threatened draw the church into the discussion and application of asylum and refugee policy. It is inevitable, especially perhaps in a secularized society, that this encounter between the church as a symbol of hope and the state as the bearer of responsibility for applying the law will be a continuing source of tension.

In itself, such tension is not unhealthy in the life of a democratic country. Forming or enforcing law is not a simple objective fact, but a passionate search for the best solutions in terms of the complex array of factors involved in a given situation. A dramatic action, a symbol, presenting a facet of the problem with a sense of popular drama — all these contribute to the total wisdom of society in solving problems that are at hand. It is logical that the state should be more sensitive than the church to public opinion, more respectful of legal definitions, for it has a sense of responsibility for the whole of society, economically, culturally and politically. In a sense, administration and expediency are paramount for the state. Of course, state functionaries include many sensitive persons (among them persons with strong Christian convictions) who are trying to do their best under the circumstances in which they find themselves. It is sometimes difficult for them to avoid conflicts between their personal Christian consciousness, operating within the framework of political realities, and the collective opinion of a church or a group of Christians who operate outside those constraints and are specifically motivated by concrete cases of human need in which they are trying to help.

The temptation of the state is to claim total authority as representative of the whole society. The temptation of the church is to affirm its obedience to God in contradiction to its relation to the authorities. We will be ill served if all go on in polemic terms claiming their own territory and points of reference and forgetting that the fundamental criterion is the protection of the weak and the extension of help to people in difficult situations. The challenge to all is to find the best human solutions to the concrete problems we confront. For this, collaboration between the state, as representing all sectors of society, and the churches is necessary. We should not assume that confrontation must be the norm in church-state relations. On the contrary, in many areas — including reception, social adjustment, provision of housing — there is a great deal which can be done together.

A second dimension of the relationship between church and state is that of questioning and dialogue. Not all partners in the discussion about shaping or applying law have the same perspectives, experiences and expertise. Data must be compared with data to make possible mutual correction. This can be done in a direct, private way; it can also be done through the mass media in terms of shaping public opinion. But the questioning, the dialogue, the critical remarks and positive suggestions should be seen as an integral part of the collaboration between church and state in the service of people in need.

A third dimension of this collaboration should be a clarification of the notion of the state in democracies. Under some circumstances, the apparent confrontation between church and state may be premature because the executive branch of the government has assumed to itself the representation of the whole society. In contesting decisions made by the executive, it is possible, under most democratic constitutions, to appeal to another power of the state — the courts — and eventually individual citizens may appeal to the legislative authority for reform of the law. In other words, the fact of disobedience to one branch of government does not imply that there is disobedience to the government as a whole. It may be that this disobedience allows for a better functioning of the total mechanism of a democratic state. In some countries (Switzerland is perhaps the primary example), there is even more possibility for direct appeal to the minds of the people through concrete popular initiatives to change laws or practices.

In the traditional understanding, the right to grant refuge or asylum belonged to the "prince". It was not a right of the person who is asking for asylum but the right of the prince to grant that asylum. In a democratic system the notion of "prince" has been replaced by the notion of "people". The tensions, discussions, confrontations within the total life of the people are mechanisms to shape public opinion which will provide new impulses for society as a whole to reach decisions which are, it is hoped, more humane and more liberal. The representative character of Western democracy, in which some people are elected to bear responsibilities on behalf of the whole population, should never be construed as an abdication by the people of the right to participate fully and to make their voice heard through the normal mechanism of the law, through the available mass media or through dramatic and symbolic actions that highlight before the conscience of society the human dimensions at stake in administrative decisions.

The fundamental criterion in church-state relations is service to people in need. Confrontation is never an end in itself. The situation of refugees must not be used as an instrument in internal political struggles. The confrontations of power between loyalty to the law and loyalty to conscience, between the higher authority of the state and the highest authority of God, must never obscure the actual concrete need we all want to meet.

A final note on obedience and disobedience to the state. There is a long Christian tradition of civil disobedience, and it would be very difficult for the church to give up this possibility, of which there are clear examples in the New Testament. But the corollary to civil disobedience is willingness to pay the price in suffering that accompanies these situations. We do not claim a position above the law. We do claim the obligation of both Christians and churches to disobey the law in circumstances when a conflict of conscience cannot be solved by simple accommodation. At this moment, the willingness to pay the price imposed by society will be the best appeal to the conscience of that society. It is not the purity of our action that we are trying to protect; it is the needs of people searching for protection we are trying to serve.

Refugees have always been a source of blessing to the nation that has received them. The Acts of the Apostles describes persecuted Christians who escaped for their lives and were received in different communities in the Middle East where they became the bearers of the gospel of Jesus Christ, bearers of the notion that love is the greatest reality of all. For more than a century Latin America has received thousands and thousands of political and economic migrants from Europe. They have preserved their culture and have contributed greatly to our cultural, economic and social development. Poor people who came to us from Switzerland and Germany and Italy, searching for a new chance in life, have become a source of blessing for all of the inhabitants of the country. Can we not dream that a similar blessing will take place in the richest countries of Europe and North America?

Let us remember the flux of history symbolized by Egypt and its change from an oppressive to a protective country. Let us remember that those who today are asylum-seekers could tomorrow be those who receive *our* children in need of protection and a new chance in life.

Finally, let us remember with the writer of the letter to the Hebrews to "welcome the strangers in your home. There were some who did that and welcomed angels without knowing it. Remember those who are in prison and that you were in prison with them. Remember those who are suffering and that you were suffering as they are".

VII

Reconciliation

After having visited townships, hospitals and bereaved families in South Africa, after having come face to face with the reality of the blind violence which continues to exact more and more sacrifice from the same poor, marginalized and powerless people who have been paying the price of apartheid for many years, one needs to be very courageous to speak about reconciliation.

Or when one thinks of Latin America, where the Indians were destroyed by the invasion and occupation 500 years ago, and black Africans were brought as slaves to replace the dying Indian population in the cane sugar plantations, how does one talk about reconciliation?

But what, then, shall we do with the gospel of Jesus Christ, which obliges us to believe in reconciliation? That is our difficulty. If we could only set aside the heritage of historic power relationships — the history of white people being the guardians of blacks in South Africa, the history of colonizers and colonized in Latin America and elsewhere in the world — we might solve the problem of reconciliation. But of course we cannot escape from history so easily.

As Christians we believe that God was in Christ to reconcile the world to himself, and that God has entrusted to us a ministry of reconciliation. We may have different doctrinal interpretations of the cross of Jesus Christ, but all currents of Christian spirituality coincide in seeing the cross as God's ultimate attempt to overcome human alienation. And on that cross, from the side of the victims and in identification with the oppressed, Jesus pronounced the words of forgiveness: "Father, forgive them, for they know not what they do."

So this is our dilemma: a reality that makes reconciliation impossible and a vision, a conviction, a promise and an obligation that make reconciliation available. How do we bridge the gap between the vision and the reality?

I want to begin by looking at some passages in the Bible that can perhaps shed some light on our dilemma. We are aided by the fact that the Bible is a very down-to-earth book. It speaks of life as it is. The writers of the Bible knew that to speak of reconciliation is sometimes a luxury that must wait for a while. Remember the family quarrel between Abraham and Lot recorded in Genesis 13. Quarrels had broken out between the two families, and when they degenerated into violence, Abraham said, "Wait a minute. Let us make a practical arrangement. If you go to the left, I will go to the right. If you go to the North, I will go to the South. But let us not quarrel. There is plenty of land."

That was *not* reconciliation. For reconciliation you need to embrace; you need to love each other. Abraham's suggestion went along another line: "Let us first avoid war. Let us assure life. Let us first be certain that we preserve the possibility of talking later about deeper things." Until life, as a gift of God, is a privilege that is recognized for every child of God, there is no way to begin speaking of reconciliation. The society that looks forward to the possibility of reconciliation has the prior task of assuring life for all citizens, ensuring minimum dignity for all and guaranteeing that people may come with free will to speak of reconciliation, and not simply be obliged to accept solutions imposed on them because they are too weak to resist. First, assure life.

A second biblical paradigm of reconciliation is found in Genesis 32 and 33. It is the story of the encounter, after a long separation, of the two brothers Jacob and Esau. Jacob is the clever, dishonest fellow who managed by trickery to claim the primacy and blessing of his father which rightfully belonged to his older brother. Warned by his mother that Esau was about to kill him, Jacob escaped abroad. Twenty years later, he decided to return. But he was afraid. He knew what he had done. Twenty years can be time enough to forgive and forget, but it can also be the time to stoke your anger to a white heat.

Out of fear Jacob organized a strategy to pave the way for approaching his brother. He began to send messages: "The Lord has blessed me. I will come back to you, my lord." He had received the primacy, but he also recognizes the primacy of his brother. In all he sent seven committees with gifts to try to tame Esau. Esau, beautiful soul, wanted to embrace his brother, but the guilty one was not convinced that it would be possible. So he prepared the way for potential reconciliation by a restitution of part of what he had taken from his brother and by inclining himself in reverence seven times in front of his brother, to recognize his primacy in the family.

We have no idea whether or not Jacob had good intentions. But the Bible is not interested in exploring intentions at this point. It is interested only in describing the process by which two persons came close to each other and the possibility of a reconciliation that was available.

In the light of the same realism of the Bible we see in the parable of the Prodigal Son (Luke 15) what can be done to advance towards potential reconciliation even with selfish motivations. This young man got his share of the inheritance from his father and went out and enjoyed himself. Once there was no more money, he discovered he had no more friends. He was taking care of the pigs and eating like and with them. And one day he said, "I am stupid. Here I am, living this way, and look what is going on in the house of my father. The work is better there, the food is better. So I will go back to my father and say, 'Father, I am not worthy, but make me one of your workers.'"

The Prodigal Son had his own salvation plan, his own strategy. It did not involve repentance. He was not concerned about the pain he had inflicted on his father. He only wanted to eat — which is of course a legitimate concern. So, out of very poor motivation, he came close to the father. The father came running to him and embraced him. In the father's forgiveness the son realized the magnitude of his sin. He could propose no solution. He could only say, "I have sinned against heaven and against you." But he could say that only in the presence of the forgiving love of his father.

Sometimes we say, "repent, in order to be forgiven." But the real repentance comes when we *are* forgiven. It is only when we see the love of a wife who forgives an unfaithful husband that we see the magnitude of his action. It is only in this moment of spiritual embrace that one comes close to what is called reconciliation. Before that, through envy or contention, through good or bad intentions, the Prodigal Son was walking towards his father and Jacob was walking towards his brother.

There is an interesting sidelight to the story of Jacob's encounter with Esau. In the middle of the biblical account we read the well-known episode of Jacob's wrestling with a stranger at the riverside. At daybreak, when the man asks to be let go, Jacob refuses to do so until he receives a blessing. In the light of this experience, he names the place Peniel — "the face of God" — because, he reflects, "I have seen God face to face, and yet my life is preserved." Then he continues on the road to meet his brother; and after Esau embraces him and forgives him, he is able to say, "Truly to see your face is like seeing the face of God."

The Bible and the churches have spoken about conversion as one way to reconciliation. But conversion by itself is not enough for reconciliation. Conversion is the change of attitudes that puts me face to face with my neighbour, with the victims, with those whose attitude to me will be the real mediation of God's forgiveness and potential reconciliation.

Theologically we might put it this way. In the case of Jesus Christ, he as the victim was able to mediate restitution and forgiveness, even for those who had victimized him. "Father, forgive them, for they know not what they do." So, too, the father's embrace of the Prodigal Son and Esau's embrace of Jacob represent a giving back of a lost humanness, which can only be given through the victim, and which is fundamental if reconciliation is to take place.

In the recent political debate in South Africa, there has been a good deal of talk about how restitution, a means by which those who were responsible for the situation, those who have profited from apartheid, the guilty ones, can be obliged to pay the others back for what they have suffered, is necessary in order for it to be possible to begin to talk about reconciliation.

But the victim is not only a recipient of restitution. The victim is also the one who has the key to a real and fundamental reconciliation, because it is in the victim that Jesus Christ is present. It is in these people that God's intention for real humanness is manifested. So reconciliation comes at the end of a road, after you have taken steps, from different motivations, after you have come close to your neighbour, in relation to whom you recognize your guilt, after you have begun to give an indication of the seriousness of your approach. When you are embraced by those who are your former victims, then there is a chance for real building of a new fellowship, a new communion and a new community.

Remember the story in Luke 19 of Zacchaeus, the chief tax collector who climbed a tree "to see who Jesus was". The gospel does not give us any information about the conversation when Zacchaeus went to dine with Jesus. But he came out from that meal with a strange public confession. "I will give to the poor and I will repay four times what I have stolen." Then Jesus announced, "salvation has come to this house."

Protestants and Catholics have quarrelled for centuries about whether salvation is by faith or by works. In fact, of course, we are saved by pure grace, because neither our faith nor our works are enough. But the point in this story is that the objective action or restitution by Zacchaeus is the evidence of what his conversion meant and of his willingness to be in reconciliation. It is the social manifestation of the internal reality which happened to him in his conversation with Jesus.

Of course, it is not a simple matter to move from the biblical, theological context to the contemporary political scene. In the Bible, with some exceptions, conflict and reconciliation take place in a face-to-face situation between individuals. And that is relatively easy to grasp: "I could forgive him" — and vice versa. It is quite different when I belong to a social group that has been collectively guilty or collectively exploited. My attitude of individual forgiveness is not enough and is not complete until I come along with my family or my people to that possibility of reconciliation.

A senior ecumenical leader has said, "I don't have any problems accepting forgiveness of my own sins. But I do not know how to accept forgiveness for my sin of being white, of being a member of a racial group that has profited from the exploitation of so many other nations in the world, and continues to profit from the structure of economic relations in the world. How can I accept forgiveness when the cause of my sin, the sin of my nation as a whole, is still in operation?"

The only response is to begin to walk like Jacob, like the Prodigal Son. Come with your guilt, but let us put ourselves on the side of the downtrodden, on the side of the marginalized, in order to try to reverse the meaning of history. We cannot change past history, but we can change the significance of that history for this and future generations.

In fact the situation in South Africa today confronts the churches with a serious temptation. The temptation is to be neutral in order to be able to help with reconciliation. The churches have been able to help in calling together all parties to the negotiating table, and public acknowledgement of their role has come as a result. But precisely here lies the danger. This public acknowledgement of the churches' role should never be a recognition of a supposed neutrality between oppressed and oppressors. That cannot be the stance of the church of Jesus Christ, who took to himself the destiny of the downtrodden of his time and who forever walks through the world embracing the children and the powerless.

The church may not pretend to be above the tragedies. Politically speaking, it is not possible to remove the guilt of individuals, and it is not possible to remove the guilt of the church. I cannot assume the lofty stance of pointing the finger and saying that only the Dutch Reformed Church is guilty of apartheid, for that is my church as much as the Methodist Church is my church. I cannot say that what was done to the indigenous people in Latin America was done by only the Catholic Church, because it was done in the name of the Bible and in the name of the Lord Jesus Christ whom I worship. We need to acknowledge this collective guilt and let that acknowledgement motivate all of us to enter into the struggle on the side of the downtrodden to overcome the situation.

Moreover, the churches and all others who are concerned with the situation should think of what signposts can be planted, what indications can be given that we care for life. This is not just a matter of declarations and prophetic statements. In every local parish, in every neighbourhood, in every slum area and township, churches and other concerned people need to try to bring people together to see how it is possible to preserve life, even if only at a minimum level. We cannot proclaim a reconciliation in whose name we refuse to give a cup of water to our neighbour. We cannot dream so much of our high ideals that we lose sight of the present realities. There are pragmatic steps to take which are not easy, but which are absolutely necessary if the process is to develop.

Furthermore, we need to develop structures of conciliation, structures of conversation, structures that oblige people to talk to each other. When I met with President de Klerk, he was obliged to receive me and I was obliged to see him. But I think the kind of constraint given by what he represents and what I represent is a good constraint, because it provides the chance to demythologize, to put the problems on the table and to open the door to future possibilities on the road to a reconciliation that is far away — a reconciliation that we believe should be possible. Forums must be created in which representatives of the most varied positions in society contribute, at the political level, towards reconciliation.

Of course, we must come to the question of restitution. As we saw from the biblical accounts we cited, restitution is a sign of the honesty of the process. Restitutions is a way to guarantee and protect life, to prove your honesty and to facilitate others' perception of the honesty of your position. But restitution is also something deeper. It is the conviction that we cannot say "We have finished a page, so now we begin again from zero", without assuming the consequences from the past and creating conditions of humanness for everyone.

At one African National Congress seminar someone proposed that a tax of 30 per cent be levied on wealth to compensate somehow for the disadvantages of the majority of the people. The resulting uproar in the media demonstrated two things: that some people in South Africa are afraid of losing their privileges and that others are convinced that something needs to be done. The point is to internalize that conviction and to bring that internalization to the negotiating tables. The issue is not whether this or that idea should be accepted or rejected but to bring forward intelligent possibilities that will indicate a willingness to make restitution and to explore the possibilities involved in the processes of creating conditions for a real reconciliation.

What is the role of the church in all this? Its first task is to shout very loudly, "Reconciliation is possible! Do not give up! Do not surrender to violence! Reject the idea that violence can be a methodology to remove or to maintain the status quo!" Such a No to violence is needed because the promise of reconciliation is there, and we believe that God's promises are stronger than our human obstacles to their fulfillment.

Second, let the church be close to the victims, to the suffering people, to keep steadying them with the hope that, even if death visits us today, it is not powerful enough to deprive those who have fallen on the road of the glory of contemplating, from the outskirts of heaven, how the life of their dear ones is being transformed for the better. That is where the church must be because it is from that perspective, and with the hope generated in that encounter with the people, that others can be embraced in a sincere and honest manner.

Finally, let the church set up signs of the potential of reconciliation by running a little faster than civil society and providing examples of potential encounters on the road to reconciliation. It cannot be that churches will change because the political parties change. It cannot be that the dreams the churches can develop are limited to the possibilities that politicians have for fulfilling them. No, the church must say in the name of our God, "Reconciliation is waiting for us. Let us begin to assure life. Let us begin to walk to the encounter with our neighbour. Let us begin to make restitution. Let us hope for the miracle that will surprise us at any moment."

VIII

Justice, Peace
and the Integrity of Creation

The Sixth Assembly of the World Council of Churches (Vancouver, 1983), called for the development of a conciliar process for justice, peace and integrity of creation (JPIC). Three basic concerns came together in shaping this fundamental emphasis of the modern ecumenical movement:

• The realization that the world as a whole was in danger. Nuclear and chemical weapons gave this generation the capacity to destroy the whole of creation. The growing gap between rich and poor and the tremendous burden of foreign debt in non-industrialized countries were condemning millions of people to early death. The ecological threat was perceived in all its terrible potentialities. These three issues were three faces of the same comprehensive human problematic.

• The need to articulate theologically our understanding of that human predicament and to spell out theologically our specific Christian responsibility. What is God's relation with nature and history? What role does our human activity play within that relation? To indicate the seriousness of our historical engagement, Vancouver put the word "covenant" in the title of this programme emphasis: within the covenant of God with creation and with humankind we need to listen to God's call for repentance and to discover meaning, relation and strength for our own historical participation. Our response as churches to the crisis posed by injustice, war and the destruction of creation was seen as a test of our basic confession that Jesus Christ is Lord and Saviour.

• The unity of the church. Within this search for conciliarity as a new avenue towards overcoming the divisions among the churches there is a double challenge: our ecclesiology should include and be tested by a reference to God's basic attitude towards creation and history; and engaging in a common process of confronting the issues of the day should help us to discover in depth the unity already existing and facilitate growing into wider unity.

The central process of reflection on JPIC was carried on by a special working group which drafted a consensus document introduced at the world convocation on JPIC in Seoul in early 1990. There it proved impossible to come to terms with the theological conceptual foundation of the whole process. Opposition came both from people in the Third World who mistrusted a fully-rounded document that they considered to be too Western in style (even if most of the drafters were themselves people from the Third World) and persons coming from churches of a more classical Western tradition of doctrinal formulation who were not happy with the concepts contained in the first part. However, if the document as such was not owned by the convocation in Seoul, the general trends — a christological incarnation approach, a new emphasis on creation and an openness to the truth experience of other religions — did permeate the minds of most participants.

Through that process of discussion ten affirmations, which are a substantial résumé of convictions held by the ecumenical movement, were agreed upon to guide participation in the search for a more human society. Four areas were highlighted as demanding a special covenanting in the present situation of the world. These four covenants are invitations to be more specific in concrete areas, where common action and networks of solidarity could be established. The main criticism levelled at this whole process is the general character of the affirmations and the headings of these covenants. We must still advance in the effort to give historical content to those affirmations and to provide specific avenues, "middle axioms" or intermediary targets where effort could be concentrated at a particular moment and in a particular place.

The Seventh Assembly (Canberra, 1991) advanced the theological reflection by providing as a frame of reference the main theme: "Come, Holy Spirit — Renew the Whole Creation". It is a prayer for the presence of the Holy Spirit that will give a sacramental character to all relations with God's creation. Through a trinitarian theology it is possible to affirm the autonomy of human and creation history and hence our responsibility for them and at the same time keep that autonomy within an understanding of God's concern, God's presence, God's providence.

While in Seoul the church was almost unavoidably conceived as a sociological reality, a people called to develop activities for the safeguard of creation, justice and peace, Canberra described the church more as a sign and symbol of God's purpose for creation, giving new importance to the priestly and intercessory role of the church. This should not be seen as opposition to or correction of Seoul, but as a foundation for that sense of participation in the struggles of the world which should manifest the reality of our calling to be in history — through repentance, denunciation and solidarity with the struggling poor — an anticipation of the kingdom to come.

The new world situation

While nothing has challenged the fundamental importance of the four areas for covenanting and the recognition of their interaction, it is obvious that dramatic changes in the world situation since Vancouver demand new analyses and will impose additional concrete responses. Perhaps a common term to characterize these new situations is "ambiguity". Of the many examples that could be given, consider the following:

• Nearly all countries in Latin America have passed from military dictatorship to a liberal style of democracy during this period. In this sense, there is real progress, but these democracies have not been able to cope with the growing impoverishment of the people.

• In Central and Eastern Europe we have witnessed a formidable expression of popular participation in reaction against rigid political and economic systems. The total collapse of the centralized socialist system brought the promise of freedom, but has created a chaotic situation in which the way into the future is difficult to perceive.

• In the southern part of Africa we have seen the independence of Namibia and the dramatic change of current in South Africa with a marvellous symbolic meaning: racism has received a tremendous blow and those who have expressed solidarity with anti-apartheid forces all over the world should feel their struggle is being rewarded. But the question of restitution and justice for the deprived masses still awaits an answer.

• The gap between North and South has continued to widen in dramatic ways. The issue has been recognized internationally, mechanisms to cope with the problem of foreign debt have been devised, GATT has carried on conversations on free trade, the IMF and the World Bank have provided recipes for adjustments to most countries. But the net result so far is enormous social costs and a growing fear in the rich countries of being confronted with a massive influx of migrants.

● There is a new awareness of the ecological crisis and a substantial change in public opinion worldwide in the perception of this issue, evident in the interest and hopes invested in the UN Conference on Environment and Development (UNCED) in Rio de Janeiro. Meanwhile, however, uncontrolled use of energy is still the rule, and international constraints are not yet in place to oblige people to comply with the basic requirements of ecological responsibility. The dominating economic paradigm functions without taking account of ecological realities, limits and values.

● The end of the Cold War has opened up a new period in world history. In the past, nuclear deterrence prevented a major war in Europe between the superpowers, but it did not prevent them from waging war against each other by encouraging local or national conflicts in many parts of the world. Today many of those conflicts remain. Some have reached a degree of violence almost unheard of — for example, in Liberia and Somalia — though they get little attention from world opinion. We could make a long list of other conflicts. Some should be interpreted as struggles of the people for liberation, but most of them are much more ambiguous, because they involve people — very often poor people — of different ethnic groups or different ideological or religious persuasions engaged in battles against each other. Other categories beyond that of economic exploitation or foreign political oppression will need to be used to interpret those conflicts and to develop strategies for peace.

● Recent developments reveal the links between environmental deterioration and war. Perhaps the most undeveloped connection in our analysis and theological understanding within JPIC is that between the integrity of creation and peace. Today, deteriorating ecological conditions are creating hundreds of thousands of environmental refugees and migrants, and are new sources of conflict and potential war. In the Middle East, for example, one of the key issues is access to and control of water.

● The expression of the feminist revolution has spread dramatically all over the world. I use the word revolution quite intentionally, because what is going on in people's consciousness, family life and cultural and political discussion is of tremendous significance for the future of humankind. It is more than the pursuit of economic and political justice. It is the affirmation of values, perspectives and experiences that are coming to the forefront of the intellectual and spiritual debate in every society.

There are certainly many other aspects of the current situation which are substantially different from what they were in 1983. But I would conclude this list by referring to changes in the situation of the churches which render more difficult the dream of a council to speak with authority on matters of justice, peace and creation. The identification of ethnic conflicts with confessional identities in Balkan and Eastern European countries has created a situation of tension among the churches that does not facilitate speaking with authority on the problems of the world. The churches are deeply involved in the ambiguities of the historical situation. The real ecumenical challenge is to keep open the lines of communication in order to see whether, in the midst of conflict, there is a commonality of vision that could be affirmed, even if we are not able to articulate ways to apply that vision in the concrete situation of conflict. The notion of conciliarity is being severely tested even as the need for it is felt more keenly.

What next?

1. Despite the overwhelming nature of the problems confronting humankind and the ambiguity of many recent historical events, one thing is clear: in the faith perspective, resurrection has the final word. We cannot accept history as a closed process because the Spirit of God is at work. Historically, faith has motivated people to resistance, endurance, perseverance, expectations of a new morning, hope. All over the world, we are witnessing a revival of religiosity and organized religion. This could be an escape from the conflicts and ambiguities of daily life, but it could also provide ways in which to help each other to survive and to work towards the new day. The vision of God's peace in the Old Testament and the coming of the kingdom in the perspective of Jesus challenge all existing realities in the light of the promise of a different tomorrow. Faith enables us to keep perceiving the goal clearly in the midst of relativities and limitations.

The JPIC covenants articulated in Seoul can be exercised in frustrating situations and in powerlessness, or in the frustrations of the exercise of power that cannot deliver at the level of our own Christian expectations. But Christian hope is not to be confused with optimism or utopianism. It knows the ugly reality of sin in the cross of Jesus Christ, but it is even more aware of the power released in the resurrection of Jesus Christ and of God's faithfulness in life and in eternity.

2. Our theological task should include a new consideration of our epistemological situation. The notion of conciliarity should apply from the outset to the processes of analysis and interpretation. In recent years new theological systems have claimed to bring forward the fruits of the experience of particular groups in dealing with the teaching of the Bible and the reading of modern reality. Minjung theology in Korea and liberation theology in Latin America include a particular *epistemological* option for the poor as those who, in their powerlessness, are able more clearly to grasp God's judgement and promises. Something similar could be said of the newly affirmed and life-centred theological vision of women.

Our theological generation has inherited the legacy of those masters of suspicion, Marx, Freud and Nietzsche, who invited us to look beyond the articulation of words and phrases to the actual ideological positions, psychological conditioning and power relations in which people find themselves. I mentioned that at the Seoul convocation many Third World delegates could not accept the document presented at face value because they suspected that underlying conscious or unconscious categories of thought of the rich world were being smuggled in through it. Women are also tempted to follow the same pattern in their participation in the theological debate, suspecting *a priori* the male, patriarchal content of our theological formulations.

But we claim to be members of the Body of Christ. We claim to have a common world of reference in the revelation of God in the message of the Bible. This means that, despite our different social, economic, political and ideological presuppositions, we share a commonality of being in the sacramental life of the church, which is a given of the epistemological situation.

The ecumenical insistence on the preferential option for the poor in the gospel of Jesus Christ as the central yardstick for judging any particular social situation does not mean to sacralize the epistemological position of the poor. The poor are within different ideological systems and sometimes come to conflicting proposals. Among the poor there are those who are not recognized by others who are economically or politically powerless — poor women, for example, or poor ethnic and racial minorities. Their perspective, too, must be brought to the total debate. In the Bible and in the history of the church, there are testimonies to the experience of the poor of yesterday which could enrich our search for truth and interpretation today.

There is also the service rendered by the accumulation of scientific knowledge. Of course, scientific knowledge, especially in the social sciences, cannot be exonerated from ideological presuppositions, but the data elaborated are a fundamental component of all discussions on interpreting a particular reality. We should not surrender to academia or assume that only technocrats are able to run a modern society properly, but neither should we surrender to populism in a naive affirmation of some selective popular wisdom. And while we should exercise a certain suspicion in every direction, we are also called to trust out of the forgiveness and reconciliation and sacramental givenness of the church's life.

Ecumenical dynamics should provide for accountability and reciprocal correction. The preferential option for the poor is a clear indication of solidarity following the model of Jesus Christ, but our solidarity with the poor will not be honest if it does not involve all our mind and all our knowledge. Just as the love of God should embrace our soul, our heart and our mind, the love of our neighbour, too, should involve the totality of our personality, including our critical capacities.

The aim of the World Council of Churches is to bring together in a conciliar debate of correction and inspiration all sectors of the human family with their particular experience of God's revelation to them, to humankind and to the world. It is only by real participation that exchange takes place and correction can happen and easy idealizations of our particular positions can be avoided.

Sociologically speaking, most of the synods and assemblies of our historic churches are in the hands of male persons beyond middle age. They rely heavily on the trust relations provided by the sacramental unity in the church. This is a traditional value that should not be taken lightly. But at the same time, those decision-making bodies need to be questioned with a view to their conciliarity with all other sectors of the people of God so that their deliberations incorporate, even if second-hand, the experience, perspectives and insights of the others.

In any case, as we look at decision-making processes and the reading of concrete historical situations, whether in the ecumenical movement as a whole or in the concrete situation of our local communities, let us keep alive both suspicion and trust, both commonality of belonging and awareness of our own dependency on the values of the class or group to which we belong. It is only in the cross-fertilization of these two components that the Bible can be opened to shed light on the complexities and ambiguities of our present history.

3. A conciliar process of investigation and interpretation should aim at formulating alternatives to the prevailing reality which are *possible*. Since its First Assembly the WCC has been critical of the two great economic and socio-political systems. Now the socialist regimes in Central and Eastern Europe have collapsed, partly because Marxist anthropology concentrated so much on eliminating classes that it did not perceive the growing corruption that power produced precisely in those who were supposed to be the avant-garde in the new society. The overall impression is that the market system has triumphed. But we from the Third World know that there is no such thing as a free market. Try to stop the subsidy for farm exports in Western countries and see how free the market is! Or try to sell sugar in the United States!

The market is the best way found so far to multiply production to respond to the demands of purchasers. It has not been designed to respond to the demands of poor human beings. Nor has socialism or capitalism been able to respond to ecological challenges or to point a way out of the crisis of inner-city life. We should neither contemplate the collapse of the socialist regimes with nostalgia nor idolize the market system. As a community we must enter into the process of designing possible alternatives in which the values of the market as a system of exchange could be preserved but put at the service of the totality of the population.

A reading of the ten affirmations of Seoul should be helpful in providing a sense of direction and a set of challenges to any model of society proposed. We need to recover the search for a society that is "sustainable" in two senses: "*able* to be sustained", that is, with ecological responsibility for the coming generations, but also "*worthy* of being sustained", that is, ensuring that the quality of humanity within that society inspires the loyalty of all its members. We must find our way between the realism of the givenness of human limitations and constraints and the utopia of the kingdom of God. I cannot find a better expression for the society we are looking for than a *caring* society, in which whatever competition is demanded by the economic system is softened, supported, humanized by a tissue of human relations and protective structures that constitute a permanent jubilee year, a permanent new beginning, a permanent rehabilitation of people from the periphery or marginalization into a manifold process of participation, support, restoration.

By affirming a sustainable society we run the risk of affirming the relativism of the prevailing ideology of pragmatism in terms of what is possible within human parameters as the maximum aspiration of a given society. While we recognize the freedom given to human beings in creation, and with that freedom the autonomy over political decisions, this freedom and this autonomy need to be conceived within a theological frame of reference that invites us to use it responsibly and accountably towards the aims of the kingdom to come. In that way, our historical decisions, as they incorporate our love for neighbour in structural and behaviour forms, express the degree of seriousness of our love for God because, according to Jesus, the second commandment is similar to the first commandment. With the same seriousness with which we consider as heresies those opinions concerning God that do not reflect the basic convictions of Christian tradition, we are entitled to consider heretical all attitudes in relation to neighbour which do not emanate from expressions of love, responsibility and care for every creature. Trinitarian theology provides us with a model to understand the right relation between freedom and accountability in the sense of belonging. While recognizing the ambiguous and penultimate character of all our historical decisions, we see within them the values of the ultimate which are at stake.

4. The JPIC process is a call not only to reflect on the meaning of God's covenant with humanity, but also to respond to that covenant in our solidarity and reciprocal support. Perhaps the struggle against apartheid in South Africa has been the best example of this solidarity, this belonging to the covenant of God, in terms of both the particular struggle carried on by the people and the churches in South Africa and the international network of solidarity groups who have shared in the faith commitment of the South African people and made that struggle their own. While their solidarity has obviously been manifested in economic sanctions and the formation of public opinion, its fundamental value is in the moral-ethical-theological recognition that it was an integral part of belonging to the covenant for justice that God has shaped for all humanity in Jesus Christ.

That model should help us to understand, appreciate and be thankful for the many similar instances of people coming together to confront issues of peace or justice or ecological responsibility. With the tragic multiplication of local conflicts in the post-Cold War period, new strategies must be discovered by peace groups. In many countries, covenants could be made engaging the community to defend asylum-seekers in a climate of growing xenophobia and rejection of foreigners. It is very important to plant signs of hope, to strengthen networks of support and to create, not islands of retreat from the world, but centres of renewal, of new potential, of new vision. Canberra drew attention to the need to strengthen the civil society, to multiply groups of reciprocal support and inspiration. Local parishes are invited to become what they are supposed to be in God's plan: communities of healing, centres of human renewal.

One of the most moving moments at Seoul was the witnessing and celebrating of specific "covenants" made there between various groups and churches from different countries. Twenty such examples were shared at Seoul; these could be multiplied into twenty thousand.

If the church is a sign and sacrament of God's particular care for creation, it follows that how we as Christian communities engage in history manifests the degree of our ecclesial reality. By being together, planting signs, being symbols, reflecting the sacramental reality of God's love for the world, we are expressing a unity that needs to be recognized for what it is, a conciliar reality, a belonging together inside God's covenant which has ecclesial significance.

We must not allow contradictions between the search to over-come doctrinal differences and articulate the common faith and the reality of living out that commonality of faith in concrete manifesta-tions of our love of God in our neighbour which is also a confession of our faith. A normal component of conciliar fellowship should be the consideration of the social and ethical options that are opening up in our ecumenical pilgrimage. The affirmation of the equal dignity of all human beings, regardless of the colour of their skin, is not an option, but a faith affirmation that belongs to our being church and to our search for the unity of all churches. The preferential option for the poor is a given of the gospel and a non-negotiable of our ecclesial reality. The doctrinal articulation continues to be necessary to enable us to respond with all our minds in praising the unity given by God in Christ. But that doctrinal articulation will be helped by the reality of our common engagement in living out in society, under the direction of the Holy Spirit, the reality of the presence and action of the triune God in creation and history.

Those engaged in urgent historical struggles do not always have the patience, the time or the concern to discuss the consequences of their engagement for the being and unity of the church. Those concerned fundamentally with overcoming centuries-old doctrinal conflicts are inclined to fear the activism of those who would like to jump from common action in history to common affirmations about the being of the church. But it is impossible to divide what God has united. Doctrinal articulation can be of no real service to the life of the churches if it is not closely related to their missionary engagement in their being in history, their becoming signs and outposts of the kingdom to come.

5. I have deliberately concentrated on the Christian perspective of a conciliar process for JPIC, because we need to put our own house in order. But concern for the future of humankind is obviously not a province reserved for Christians. The wish to confront the problems that assail humanity and creation cannot be the monopoly of the Christian faith. We have learned a great deal from the kind of religious relation that people whom we call "aboriginal" have with earth and creation. We have a great deal to learn from the Buddhist understanding of the interdependence of all beings, and from the depth of their understanding of "being at peace". We must also be open to the correction that other religious groups bring to our historical record as Christians. But we will contribute to this common human search in a positive and constructive manner only if we carry with us both the contribution of our Christian heritage and the reality of the Christian church in the world today.

In Latin America and North America, remembrance of the 500th anniversary of the arrival of the conquerors — and later of the evangelists — makes it clear that the church has a good deal of homework to do in confronting that history, in highlighting the dimension of repentance and in showing how the present generation can covenant with the marginalized and the powerless in order to redeem that yesterday and to project a new reality for today and tomorrow. But this cannot be done without an attempt to recover something of the spirituality of the aboriginal inhabitants of Latin America and of the richness the black population brought with them from Africa and developed since then. Our role is to work from inside the Christian community, to open it up to recognition of others, to learning from others, to reconciliation with others and, we hope, to covenanting with others for the shaping of a different future.

The world of secular science and technology, the old world of religious wisdom, the different ideological configurations that compete for humankind's allegiance must also be present in our attempt to shape together a commonality of dreams for the future of society and creation. But we should come to the encounter of those worlds of thought and experience with clarity about our own identity and in a humble spirit of repentance and hope.

The situation today often makes it difficult to see openings on the horizon of humankind which could change the frustration felt by great masses of people. Understandably, we tend to develop theologies of survival and services that will help people to go through this present period with the hope that they will still be alive when history will open again and new chances may appear. I mentioned hope. A theology of faith against all odds of history is fundamental even for survival. Children are being born, God is still faithful. There are still also 7000 who have not given loyalty to Baal. In this hope the conciliar process must continue, and the Spirit will surprise us with undreamed-of possibilities.

Sources

Chapter I, "The Unity of the Church", is adapted from the general secretary's report to the WCC Central Committee meeting in Hanover, Germany, August 1988; the complete text was published in *The Ecumenical Review*, January 1989.

Chapter II, "Come, Holy Spirit — Renew the Whole Creation", is adapted from the general secretary's report to the WCC Central Committee meeting in Geneva, September 1991; the complete text was published in *The Ecumenical Review*, January 1992.

Chapter III, "Evangelism: Ecumenical Frontiers Today", is adapted from the general secretary's report to the WCC Central Committee meeting in Moscow, July 1989; the complete text was published in *The Ecumenical Review*, October 1989.

Chapter IV, "Missionary Identity and Interfaith Dialogue", is adapted from two lectures given at the Pacific School of Religion, Berkeley, California, USA, in 1988.

Chapter V, "Ecumenical Social Responsibility", is adapted from the general secretary's report to the WCC Central Committee meeting in Geneva, March 1990; the complete text was published in *The Ecumenical Review*, July-October 1990.

Chapter VI, "Christian Responsibility and Refugees", is adapted from a lecture at an ecumenical consultation on refugees and asylum, in Zurich, Switzerland, in 1986.

Chapter VII, "Reconciliation", is adapted from an address at the University of Natal, Pietermaritzburg, South Africa, in October 1991.

Chapter VIII, "Justice, Peace and the Integrity of Creation", is adapted from a lecture given at Iliff School of Theology, Denver, Colorado, USA, in 1992.